PHOTOGRAPHY YEAR

TIME
LIFE
BOOKS
®

Life World Library
Life Nature Library
Time Reading Program
The Life History of the United States
Life Science Library
Great Ages of Man
Time-Life Library of Art
Time-Life Library of America
Foods of the World
This Fabulous Century
Life Library of Photography
The Time-Life Encyclopedia of Gardening
The American Wilderness
The Emergence of Man
Family Library
    The Time-Life Book of Family Finance
    The Time-Life Family Legal Guide

PHOTOGRAPHY YEAR

1973 EDITION

BY THE EDITORS OF TIME-LIFE BOOKS

TIME-LIFE BOOKS, NEW YORK

ON THE COVER: Technological and esthetic accomplishments in photography during 1972 are both reflected in this two-part design. At the left is a photograph of a seashell taken with the new Polaroid SX-70 Land camera; superimposed over the photograph is an outline drawing of the camera itself. At right is a portrait of a young woman taken by Judy Dater, one of the outstanding new photographers of the year.

Contents

TIME-LIFE BOOKS

FOUNDER: Henry R. Luce 1898-1967

Editor-in-Chief: Hedley Donovan
Chairman of the Board: Andrew Heiskell
President: James R. Shepley
Chairman, Executive Committee: James A. Linen
Editorial Director: Louis Banks
Group Vice President: Rhett Austell

Vice Chairman: Roy E. Larsen

EDITOR: Jerry Korn
Executive Editor: A. B. C. Whipple
Planning Director: Oliver E. Allen
Text Director: Martin Mann
Art Director: Sheldon Cotler
Chief of Research: Beatrice T. Dobie
Director of Photography: Melvin L. Scott
Assistant Text Directors: Ogden Tanner, Diana Hirsh
Assistant Art Director: Arnold C. Holeywell

PUBLISHER: Joan D. Manley
General Manager: John D. McSweeney
Business Manager: John Steven Maxwell
Sales Director: Carl G. Jaeger
Promotion Director: Paul R. Stewart
Public Relations Director: Nicholas Benton

EDITORIAL STAFF FOR PHOTOGRAPHY YEAR:

EDITOR: John Paul Porter
Picture Editor: Sheldon Cotler
Text Editors: Betsy Frankel, Anne Horan
Designer: Albert Sherman
Staff Writers: Don Nelson, Suzanne Seixas,
Timberlake Wertenbaker, Johanna Zacharias
Chief Researcher: Nancy Shuker
Researchers: Elizabeth Dagenhardt,
Helen Fennell, Lee Hassig, Ruth Kelton,
Carolyn Stallworth, John Conrad Weiser
Art Assistant: Patricia Byrne

Editorial Production
Production Editor: Douglas B. Graham
Quality Director: Robert L. Young
Assistant: James J. Cox
Copy Staff: Rosalind Stubenberg,
Barbara Quarmby, Ricki Tarlow,
Florence Keith
Picture Department: Dolores A. Littles,
Gail Nussbaum

Valuable aid was provided by these individuals and departments of Time Inc.: Editorial Production, Norman Airey, Nicholas Costino Jr.; Library, Peter Draz; Picture Collection, Doris O'Neil; TIME-LIFE Photo Lab, George Karas, Herbert Orth, Albert Schneider; TIME-LIFE News Service, Murray J. Gart; Correspondents Elisabeth Kraemer (Bonn), Frank Iwama (Tokyo), Maria Vincenza Aloisi and Josephine du Brusle (Paris), Margot Hapgood, Penelope Reuter and Ray van Note (London), Ann Natanson (Rome), Alan H. Anderson Jr. and William Jeffrey Radford (Rio de Janeiro), Marsh Clark (New York), Jerome P. Curry (St. Louis), Friso Endt (Amsterdam), Traudl Lessing (Vienna), Nina Lindley (Buenos Aires), Henry Muller (Vancouver), Madeleine Nash (Chicago), John Shaw (Moscow), Eva Stichova (Prague).

Photography is a fascinatingly diverse, ever-changing, self-renewing phenomenon. During every year since it was invented in the 1820s there have been advances in technology and, almost as frequently, changes in esthetic attitudes and styles. Photographers never cease to find new ways of taking pictures and, in doing so, they incite designers and engineers to come up with new and more sophisticated films, cameras and other equipment. Furthermore, photographers are continually surprising even themselves with fresh insights and forms of expression with the equipment already at hand.

Photography is a field in which so much happens so fast that a continuing record is needed to chart its progress. That is the purpose of PHOTOGRAPHY YEAR: to keep abreast of the latest and most important developments, both the technical and the artistic, and to present a report on them annually.

The year 1972, which this edition covers, was an especially busy and fruitful one. Some remarkable advances were made in cameras and camera equipment. Major exhibitions evoked new interest in the work of photographers as disparate in styles as those of the venerable Paul Strand and the late Diane Arbus. More important photographic books were published than in any previous year. New galleries, dedicated expressly to showing and selling photographs, were opened in Rome and Vancouver, New York and Coconut Grove, Florida. And, as in every year, a number of new photographers were on the brink of recognition; PHOTOGRAPHY YEAR made a special effort, with the aid of a distinguished panel of consultants, to find the best of them and to publish a careful and representative sampling of their work.

In reporting these and other events, PHOTOGRAPHY YEAR has called on the help and expertise of the photographers and laboratory technicians of LIFE, the worldwide services of the Time-Life news bureaus, and the extensive experience of the editorial staff that produced the 17-volume *LIFE Library of Photography*.

With these resources it has been possible to produce not simply a compendium of photographs taken during 1972, but text-and-picture articles that probe the deeper meaning of events and discuss the implications that many of them portend. Thus, while the primary purpose of PHOTOGRAPHY YEAR is to report annually on recent and topical happenings, the book is also intended to be a reference work of lasting value.

The Editors

The Major Shows

For the photographer a major exhibition of his work is the greatest of coups; it bestows upon him the public recognition and—he hopes—the approbation that every artist craves. For the public an exhibition is a source of information, a means of education, possibly an index of future trends and, ideally, an esthetic experience.

Of the exhibits held in 1972—and they were legion—some were historical: the Victoria & Albert Museum in London held one during the spring called "From Today Painting Is Dead," which traced the technological and esthetic evolution of photography from the camera obscura up to the development of roll film during the 1880s. Other exhibits were topical: the announcement of President Nixon's impending visit to China and the subsequent opening of that land to the West for the first time in a quarter of a century sparked an exhibit at New York's Metropolitan Museum of Art called "Behind the Great Wall of China," a collection of various photographs taken in that country by nine different photographers. Some exhibits were retrospectives: photographers Walker Evans, Manuel Alvarez Bravo and W. Eugene Smith, all contemporary masters, were the stars of one-man shows that were displayed across the United States, Canada, Mexico and Japan. Taken together, the exhibitions of 1972 covered all manner of subjects and catered to all tastes. Among the most important were a retrospective of the work of Paul Strand (page 12), another of the late Diane Arbus (page 34) and some of the shows at the Photokina photography fair in Germany (page 46).

This Paul Strand photograph of a young French workman is one of nearly 500 included in the exhibition of his work touring the United States during 1973. In its simplicity, clarity and depth of human feeling, the picture exemplifies Strand's art at its best and most characteristic period.

Youth, Charente, France, 1951

Paul Strand at 82

Paul Strand's achievement as an artist and innovator is universally acknowledged by serious photographers, yet he was badly neglected until the major exhibition now touring the country revived interest in his work. Strand? people said. Is Paul Strand still around? Students of photography knew that 60 years ago he had struck a new note in photographic style that reverberates down to this day. Lovers of fine pictures welcomed occasional books that showed his mastery of the medium to be undiminished.

Strand, however, had somehow dropped out of the small but influential world in which reputations are made and sustained, and people thought of him more as an influential figure out of the past than as a living artist who was still doing notable work. Strand, who is now 82 and working hard in France, resists such attempts to relegate him to history. "I may be a monument," he protests, "but I'm still alive." And so he is, as his exhibition abundantly shows.

Originating in Philadelphia in late 1971, traveling to St. Louis and Boston in 1972 and going on to New York, Los Angeles and San Francisco in 1973, the exhibition demonstrates for the first time the full range and variety of Strand's work: the semiabstract pictures of machinery; the lovingly observed leaves, roots and rocks; the classic landscapes; the solemn, brooding portraits of simple people as tough and resilient as the earth they tend. The latest photographs, taken in Morocco, Ghana and Rumania between 1960 and 1967, were never shown publicly before. The earliest photographs—the New York street scenes and the semiabstract still lifes—that first won him admiration back in 1915 have not been seen in such quantity since 1945, the year The Museum of Modern Art gave him his only previous full-scale exhibition. The current show of nearly 500 pictures amply supports the view of Strand's early admirers and confirms his position as a modern master. Yet its very success raises a nagging question. If Strand is as good as he now appears to be, why was he half-forgotten for 20 years?

Strand's own explanation has the monumental simplicity of his pictures: he was neglected because photography itself was not yet well enough recognized as an art form. There is certainly some basis for this view. Even today photography has not achieved the prestige of painting, and no photographer is as well known as, for instance, Picasso. But there is more to it than that. As a young man in the first decades of this century, Strand was one of a band of embattled painters and photographers who gathered around Alfred Stieglitz in his pace-setting gallery at 291 Fifth Avenue. Stieglitz pioneered in the exhibition of photographs as works of art and introduced the art of Matisse and Picasso to America, but he thought of himself more as an artistic missionary than as a businessman and he hated the idea of mixing art and money. "I am not a salesman," he declared, when asked about his

The author of this article, Gene Thornton, is photography critic of *The New York Times* and a writer and lecturer on art and photography. A longtime student of Paul Strand's work, he interviewed Strand at his home in Orgeval, France.

In his darkroom apron, 27-year-old Paul Strand (above) was photographed in 1917 by Alfred Stieglitz at the influential "291" gallery, in which Stieglitz introduced innovative young painters, sculptors and photographers. Fifty-five years later Strand posed for Robert Haiko on a return visit to the United States for the opening of the huge retrospective exhibition of his life's work.

quarrels with potential customers, "nor are the pictures here for sale, although under certain circumstances certain pictures may be acquired." From Stieglitz, Strand learned to make a sharp division between art and commerce and, when he decided to be a photographer, he chose to devote himself to art alone.

It was not the only choice he could have made. At that time fashion photography, photojournalism and advertising photography were all getting started. Two other members of Stieglitz' group, Baron de Meyer and Edward Steichen, found ways to combine their views of art with commercial interests and went on to fame and fortune as pioneering fashion photographers for *Vogue* and *Vanity Fair*. Similarly, other photographers of talent and genius, for example, Erich Salomon, Henri Cartier-Bresson and Eugene Smith, made an art of photojournalism in publications such as *Münchner Illustrierte Presse, Picture Post* and LIFE. Strand's choice, however, was the obvious one to make in the distinctly noncommercial atmosphere that surrounded Stieglitz, and on the whole he has stuck to it.

It is true that for a few years in his youth he operated a portrait studio. Later for a decade he made a living as a newsreel movie cameraman, and later still he attempted film production. He has even made a few advertising photographs. However, as a still photographer he has on the whole avoided commerce as a saint avoids sin—whenever possible—and his last known fall from grace merely proves how right he is to do so.

It occurred in 1949 when his good friend Bill Golden, an art director for the Columbia Broadcasting System, persuaded him to photograph television antennas against the New York skyline. For the $500 fee most photographers would have managed to do the job in a day or two. Not Strand. He set up his bulky 8 x 10 view camera on the roof of a building on the East Side of Manhattan, and after studying the image in the ground glass he turned to his friend Walter Rosenblum, who had come along to help with the heavy equipment, and said, "A little too much wind today." So without taking a picture they packed up the equipment and lugged it away.

Several days later Strand and Rosenblum tried again, but this time Strand did not take a picture because he was dissatisfied with the way the sky looked. On several succeeding days they made further attempts, all unproductive; then they moved to a better location on the West Side and tried again several times without result.

"This must have gone on for six weeks, all for one stupid advertisement," Rosenblum recalls. "In the end Paul made it, of course, and it was probably the greatest picture of antennas against the New York skyline ever made. But at $500 it was not a commercial success."

Strand's choice of art over commerce was doubtless the right one for him,

13

or so this incident suggests, but it had its disadvantages. By choosing to stick to art, Strand condemned himself to making his living at other kinds of work, since there was no money in art photography, not even for a master like himself. Worse than that for a man who wanted recognition, he cut himself off from the mass media that were making other photographers famous. He confined his public appearances to books and portfolios and to occasional museum and gallery shows that seldom reach a wide audience. And that is one reason why he is not better known today.

Another reason has to do with politics. Strand's first and only photography teacher was Lewis Hine, whose deeply moving pictures of children in factories helped pave the way for child-labor legislation. Hine was just beginning his work as a crusading documentary photographer when Strand studied with him, and Strand soon drifted away to the more artistic ambit of Stieglitz. But Hine's influence lingered on, and in later years Strand found himself deeply involved in programs for social and political change. In the 1930s he came to believe that America was threatened by the machinations of reactionary big businessmen, and in the late '30s and early '40s he worked on a series of documentary films intended to alert America to the danger he saw. There was never much audience for this kind of film, and the last one he made had the bad fortune to open after America's entry into World War II had killed off what little interest there was, thus bringing Strand's movie career to an end and returning him full time to still photography.

Strand remained, however, a passionate partisan in politics. He was an active supporter of Franklin Delano Roosevelt and the Democratic Party during World War II. But when the war ended in an atomic blast over Hiroshima, followed by a cold war against Russia, he became convinced that reactionaries were once again on the march, leading America straight into Fascism and World War III. For this reason he abandoned the Democrats in 1948 and joined the third-party movement designed to put former Vice President Henry A. Wallace into the White House with a mandate to end the cold war and disarm the world.

"You know what a puritan is?" says one old friend. "Well, Paul is a Jewish puritan, which is a puritan squared. He is a man of absolutely strict principles, and you either measure up, or not." Strand measured up. His fears for America's future were not diminished when President Truman's attorney general released a list of potentially subversive organizations that included (along with the Communist Party and the Ku Klux Klan) the name of the Photo League, a workshop of documentary photographers that Strand had long served as a lecturer and adviser.

To Strand the mere existence of such a list was proof that the Fascist repression he feared had already begun, with artists like himself heading the

Six weeks of waiting for ideal weather conditions and hunting for the perfect vantage point went into the making of this photograph for an advertisement, although Strand knew he could expect only about one week's pay. The result became a two-page advertisement that ran in the September 1949 issue of FORTUNE magazine.

list of victims. And after the American people rejected Henry Wallace, Strand left the United States for Europe. He returned in 1949 when his father died, leaving him a substantial legacy, but in 1950 he moved to France for good.

There is still a mystery as to why he went. Some acquaintances believe he thought it was unsafe to stay. But Strand today has a different explanation: "Pure accident!" He says he first went to France because he was asked to do a book there (published in 1952 as *La France de Profil),* and then stayed on to do another book on Italy *(Un Paese,* 1955).

Whatever the reason, his long residence in France had the unforeseeable consequence of isolating him from America just when New York was replacing Paris as the art capital of the world, and just when photography as art was beginning to find support in America's universities. At the end of World War II few schools taught photography. However, in the boom times that followed, more and more college art departments added photographers to their staffs, until today the university is the principal patron of art photography, and the nation is flooded with photography graduates, each an ardent disciple of his master.

Strand did not need a university job—his father left him enough to live comfortably—but because of his long absence from America he never acquired the network of former students that has done so much to spread and sustain the fame of such masters and teachers of photography as Minor White and Aaron Siskind. And this is another reason why his work is not better known today.

Strand now lives in Orgeval, a village about an hour northwest of Paris, and visitors today are met at the station of Villennes-sur-Seine by a shapeless little old man all brown spots, white hair, rumpled sweaters and fingernails stained purple from darkroom chemicals. He looks more like somebody's sweet old gramps than a dangerous radical, and anyone meeting him first thinks of his age and frailty. However, Strand's faded gray-blue eyes look at the stranger with a twinkle that is perhaps more searching than humorous and, as he drives his aging station wagon up the hill from the station, honking vigorously around blind turns and through narrow, twisting streets, he inspires second thoughts about his decrepitude.

His house is a few kilometers over a hill from the station. Outside the garden wall there is a plunging view over miles of green fields and little white buildings washed in the delicate sunlight of the Île de France. The house itself, a rustic, vine-covered barn transformed into a comfortable studio and living quarters, is set in a grove of pear trees.

Hazel Strand, his third wife, comes to the door, gray-haired, grandmotherly, dressed in slacks and a sweater. She had been a staff photographer for the Red Cross when they met in 1949, but after their marriage she gave up photography because "it got too crowded in the darkroom." Now she devotes herself to making it easier for Strand to get on with his work, a full-time job that includes not only running the household—and occasionally helping out in the darkroom—but also pitching in to serve as public relations counselor when the need arises.

The setting is idyllic, and friends come out from Paris and young photographers drop by to view the Master. There is, however, trouble in paradise. Though 60 years have passed since Stieglitz and his group established the fact that photography is art, there are still doubters in the world, and Strand is apt to become testy when reminded of them. "The question of whether a photograph is a work of art is a stupid question," he says. "There is no such thing as an art, anyway. There are materials that artists work with—paint, stone, bronze—but materials aren't arts, the arts are what certain individuals do with them. So if a man chooses to use a camera and the materials of photography and can produce with these something that other people recognize as having the qualities and characteristics of art, then the question is automatically answered."

Strand's own claims to recognition rest on achievements that stretch out over more than half a century. When he was beginning, the fashion in art photography was a kind of misty impressionism, all soft focus, blurred outlines, and gauze over the lens. He himself worked that way at first, as did his associates at Stieglitz' gallery. But at the gallery he began to see the abstract works of the artists who were then revolutionizing the Paris art world—Matisse, Picasso, Braque, Brancusi—and in the summer of 1915, at his father's vacation house in Connecticut, he made a group of his own abstractions by photographing common household objects in such extreme close-up that they were sometimes unidentifiable.

These experiments, he says, taught him the elements of design and color that are fundamental to all art, and he then began to apply this lesson to the world around him. The result was "The White Fence," a picture so modern in its feeling and so free from the established conventions of photography that it became a landmark. Other photographers began to move in the same direction, and by the mid-'20s the misty, impressionist style, with its reliance on complicated darkroom manipulations, had been replaced by the sharp-focus approach that prevails today.

This innovation alone would have won Strand a place in photographic history, but his later pictures enlarged it. In the characteristic work of his maturity Strand has brought together the social concerns of Hine and the esthetic approach of Stieglitz, focusing on the lives of simple people living in backward or isolated parts of the world: provincial Mexico in the 1930s, a desolate island of the Outer Hebrides, the peasant villages of modern Egypt.

Taken in 1916 in Port Kent, New York, "The White Fence" was pivotal both in Strand's career and in the development of photography. Strand converted this common sight into an abstraction of light and dark patterns. He defied current fashion by taking the picture in sharp focus rather than in the soft, misty style then popular.

Many of these pictures are portraits of individuals. In others he shows his sitters with the hand-worn tools of their livelihood, the houses they and their forefathers have lived in, the countryside that supports them and that they in turn nurture and care for.

These calm and classic pictures, with their stoic, almost elegiac mood, sometimes seem old-fashioned to younger photographers. Strand has also been criticized for repetitiveness, since for more than 40 years he has taken the same kinds of pictures, even though in different locations. And though he thinks of himself as a realist, marching arm in arm with the plain people of the world toward a better future, he has been charged with a kind of idealism —a proletarian idealism, perhaps—for overlooking such ugly realities as the flies of Egypt.

All these criticisms are accurate as descriptions of his work, and yet somehow beside the point. For out of his few and commonplace materials, Strand has realized a classic vision of a better world than the one we know, a world in which simple people can live out their lives in peace and dignity, unharassed by wars and distant powers, subject only to mortality and the other universal rhythms of nature.

This vision may be only a dream. It may even be a frayed and tattered dream, dragged in the mud of power politics. But it is a dream as old as civilization and one without which mankind could hardly have survived. The artist who has so perfectly realized it with the camera and the materials of photography has a right to feel that he has measured up.   *Gene Thornton* ☐

Man-Made Objects

Out the Back Window, New York, 1924

Paul Strand's photographs of houses, tools and other man-made objects are often suffused with a deep feeling for the people who make and use them. At other times, however, his approach to such objects is almost abstract, and the objects are of interest only for their appearance, not for their purpose or their use by people. The same contrast between a sense of abstract design and a sense of humanity can be seen in his pictures of people *(pages 24-29)* and nature *(pages 30-33).*

His photographs of machines are especially abstract. It is often difficult to tell just what kind of machine is being depicted or even how large it is. Old-fashioned household and farming devices, however, which are shaped to the size of the human body and worn smooth by human hands, are more often photographed with a feeling for the people who use them.

When photographing houses Strand sometimes closes in on the elements of a structure—such as the rectangular apartment house sections at left—and sometimes backs away to take in a whole house or group of houses. He never photographs famous palaces or magnificent churches; he prefers the simple homes of workers and farmers. Yet his pictures of these humble dwellings have the monumental dignity of much larger and grander buildings.

Bold, angular patterns and striking contrasts of dark and light dominate this scene of New York buildings. No people are visible here, and the abstract design distracts attention from the sunless windows and the blank view they give.

After Rain, Luzzara, Italy, 1953

Here, in contrast to the picture opposite, the presence of people is strongly felt even though none are seen. It is even possible to guess what kind of people they are. The umbrella left open to dry is broken, but it is still in use. The crude wooden shutters are rotting, but a worn scrub brush is secreted in the wall by the window, and pails for water are on the sidewalk. The people here are poor, but they have not given up.

White Shed, Gaspé, 1929

The windowless walls and stark, rectangular
shapes of the sheds and houses in a Gaspé
fishing village make a bold pattern against the
lowering sky. Yet they also suggest the closed-in,
difficult lives of the simple farmers and fishermen
who live in a cold, inhospitable northern land.

No subject could be simpler than a wooden latch ▶
on a shed door, yet every element of this picture
expresses the character of old New England: the
rugged, splintery surfaces of the unpainted wood,
the plain and utilitarian shape of the latch, even
the firmness with which the door is shut.

Latch, Vermont, 1944

The Double Akeley Camera, New York, 1922

Ranchos de Taos Church, New Mexico, 1931

◄ *The motion-picture camera at left is one that Strand himself used for 10 years as a freelance newsreel cameraman. The mechanism shown is an external slow-motion gear attachment, but it was photographed primarily for its abstract beauty. The strong vertical lines, the circular motif and the brilliantly contrasted areas of light and shadow combine to make a striking composition.*

This is the back of an old mission church in New Mexico, but the bold buttress and the rugged windowless walls give it the air of a fortress —which mission churches in the Southwest often were. The front view of the church is more conventional, but it does not make nearly such a fine design for the camera, and it is much less evocative of the dangers of frontier life.

Portraits of People

The quintessential Strand photograph, someone once said, is a portrait of a peasant standing in front of a rough-hewn, weather-beaten wall, staring as though carefully posed. There is some truth to this description, for whether Strand concentrates on one or two people, or photographs a crowd, his pictures of people usually have a portraitlike calm and formality. When he was young he experimented with catching people unawares, and both then and in recent years he has occasionally photographed crowds of people. But he never takes action shots or anecdotal pictures, or even pictures of people feeling or expressing a violent emotion. Even when he catches people off guard they often seem to be posing.

Strand has photographed celebrated artists and intellectuals, but his best and most characteristic pictures have been made of obscure and humble fishermen, farmers and artisans. Though cast in the portrait form, these pictures of simple working people are not so much studies of individual character as they are symbols of man and his fate. They celebrate man's essential worth and dignity, his ability to survive misfortune and eventually to overcome all obstacles in his path.

This candid shot of a man sitting on a New York park bench was taken early in the photographer's career and it is as close as Strand ever came to capturing an informal, unposed effect. Despite the derby hat and the carefully buttoned vest, the man has a seedy, disreputable air, and he is looking over his shoulder in suspicion and distrust.

Man In a Derby, New York, 1916

Day Laborer, Luzzara, Italy, 1953

Characteristic of Strand's mature work is this
formal study of an Italian worker. The man is
unshaven, his face is creased with toil, and he
wears the cloth cap of the European working man.
But he looks steadily at the world, conscious of
his worth and probity, and he has an expression
of unshakable determination and fortitude.

Couple, Rucar, Rumania, 1967

Four Women, Essaouira, Morocco, 1962

◄ *This young Rumanian man and his wife, casually standing against a farm fence, suggest a life of confidence. The man wears factory-made clothes, but his wife still owns a traditional peasant jacket. Perhaps it is merely the novelty of being photographed, but perhaps—on the other hand —it is pride in the farm and his wife's pretty clothes that makes the man break into a smile.*

This Moroccan scene conveys the romantic air of picturesque mystery that European and American artists often find in the veiled woman of the Mohammedan East. However, Strand's principal interest seems to be the design created by the clash of darks and lights, which divide the seated figures from one another and unite them with the ground and the wall behind them.

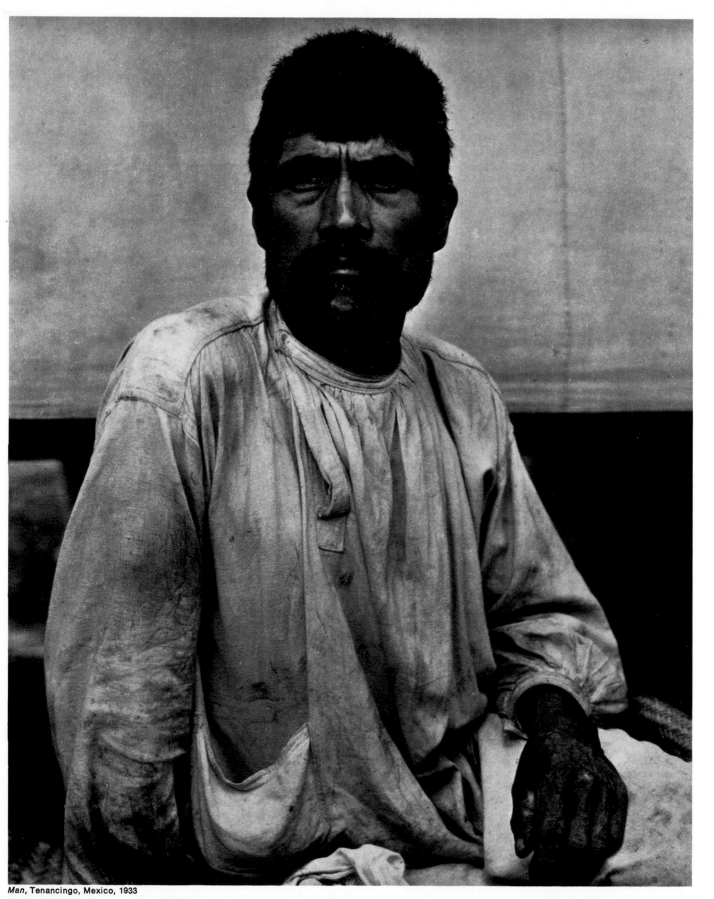

Man, Tenancingo, Mexico, 1933

The worn blouse and gnarled
fingers of this Mexican workingman
reveal the years he has spent
working with his hands—perhaps
weaving the furniture for which his
village is noted. However, he sits
erect and proud, master of his spirit
if not of his fate, and his eyes
seem to ask the ultimate question:
to what end, for what purpose, why?

Two fishermen of a small town on *Lake Pátzcuaro*, Mexico, lounge in front of a mud brick house. It is Sunday and their unadorned cotton clothes are clean. Behind them, however, there is a suggestion of countless sad centuries of poverty, toil and disease, and their dark and somber eyes and unsmiling faces seem to be gazing into eternity.

Men of Santana, Lake Pátzcuaro, Mexico, 1933

Forms and Patterns of Nature

Dunes, Abiquiu, New Mexico, 1931

*Abstract patterns made by sand, sky and
sagebrush are the real subject of this picture
of the New Mexican desert. The subtly modulated
grays of the sand, accented here and there with
spots of black, culminate in a strange cone-
shaped dune. The shining whites of the clouds, so
delicately varied in themselves, are bracketed
between a dark sky and the still darker dune.*

Strand employs two basic approaches in photographing nature: the close-up and the long shot. He rarely makes any views in between. His close-ups are very close and almost abstract: a clump of leaves *(right),* the rock textures. Long shots are very long with an epic grandeur: clouds over a sagebrush-dotted desert *(left),* a bleak seacoast.

Some of the nature pictures include buildings, domestic animals, cultivated fields, fences and other signs of man's presence and of his need for nature as the source of his very life. Others, however, are markedly empty of people. Some of the handsomest landscapes have been photographed in desert regions where man cannot live, while the close-ups of nature are almost invariably of flowers, roots or rocks that man can neither eat nor build with.

Strand's artistic vision is centered on man and the possibilities of human life. Yet in the end his pictures of nature reveal a love of nature over and above its usefulness to mankind, a love of nature for its own sake and for the sake of the forms and patterns it produces.

This close-up view of nature is also an exercise in abstract design rather than a scientific document or a record of natural beauty. Yet the bold and striking shapes of the bent iris leaves suggest the rude vitality of nature. The highlights stand out in sharp contrast to the picture's darkest shadows, and the crisscross patterns of the leaves generate a feeling of restless, thrusting activity.

Iris, Georgetown, Maine, 1928

The bare rocks and cold seas of the bleak and ▶
desolate northern coast of a Scottish island do
not seem a likely setting for man. Yet the lonely
buildings and patient horses reveal his presence.
The harsh grandeur of the landscape suggests the
effort that man must make to survive here, but it
also suggests the greatness of his achievement.

The ceaseless action of the sea has worn these
rocks smooth and revealed a pattern of thin white
lines and light-absorbing dark gray surfaces.

Rock by the Sea, Georgetown, Maine, 1927

Tir A'Mhurain, Outer Hebrides, 1954

The Life Work of Diane Arbus

When she died a suicide in July 1971 at the age of 48, Diane Arbus was already something of a cult among critics and young photographers. But during her lifetime her pictures appeared in only three major exhibits, and in those she shared the walls with other photographers. It was not until 1972 that art museums began to show the work of this enigmatic and perceptive interpreter of the world to a wide public. An exhibit of some 125 of her photographs opened at The Museum of Modern Art in New York in November, and will be seen in other United States cities later. This large show was only one posthumous honor of many. Last summer 10 of her photographs were hung at the Venice Biennale, a 77-year-old international art exhibit that had never shown photographs before. Still other exhibits devoted exclusively to her work are scheduled to follow in Paris and in Tokyo during 1973.

This newly important woman was a mysterious, wrenlike creature, as elusive during her lifetime as the power of her strange photographs is today. She was born into a well-to-do New York family and married at 18 to photographer Allen Arbus, with whom she ventured into fashion photography. After winning two Guggenheim Fellowships, in 1963 and 1966, to pursue photography as an art, she struck out on her own. The result was a haunting gallery of pictures that evade precise description. For what it pleased Diane Arbus to photograph, in the few years remaining to her, were eccentrics. Many were people who, though nominally quite ordinary, seemed strange in the context of their pictures. Others plainly lived apart from the mainstream of society, some through choice, some through fate, some because of aberrations of birth or psychology.

Her subjects included twins and triplets, giants and midgets, homosexuals and transvestites, retarded people and lonely widows. Anybody and everybody who was different drew her attention: she called such people the "silent minorities," and in case some of them should slip her mind before she got around to photographing them, she kept lists of them on a blackboard over her bed. When she focused her camera on the "normal" people of American society, she caught them engaged in the rituals with which they vary the routines of daily living. She was fascinated by contestants of all kinds, and many of her photographs record the winners of beauty contests, muscle contests, dancing contests, old folks' contests. But she also found this same sense of exotic ritual in wedding parties, cocktail parties, masked balls and Yuletide celebrations—all photographed as though by an anthropologist studying the mysterious rites of a newly found tribe.

Her curiosity, which seems to have been unquenchable, was not the curiosity of a voyeur; it was more like that of a precocious child demanding to know the reasons why. Thus the most freakish of her subjects escape the taint of sideshow exhibits. When she was asked once during a radio interview to explain herself, she answered: "When you grow up your mother says, 'Wear rubbers or else you'll catch cold.' When you become an adult you discover that you have the right not to wear rubbers and to see if you catch cold or not. It's something like that." On another occasion she uttered the melancholy plaint that "Nothing is ever the same as they said it was."

While she was obsessed with testing her own hypotheses, she was also happy to share her findings. She occasionally lectured at photography classes held at some of the art schools in the East, and a few months before she died she conducted a workshop in her own studio. One member of the class remembers that she would dart about the room, holding her hands as if grasping a camera, telling the students how she would arrange a scene in her viewfinder—and if the scene did not look just right she would shake the imaginary camera, as though that operation would make a scene rearrange itself, like the pieces in a kaleidoscope.

The young may have been the first to appreciate Arbus because they felt in her a rapport with their own defiance of what is established as the normal order of things. But there is more to her art than mere rebelliousness. Her photographs provoke contradictory readings, and her own titles, which are used beneath the nine pictures reproduced on the following pages, are no clue to her intent—they state the obvious so flatly that they suggest a deeper, hidden meaning. Arbus' photographs have been called grotesque and pitiable, hostile and compassionate, frightening and amusing; bizarre if they depict ordinary people and ordinary when they depict the bizarre. It is this susceptibility to contrapuntal interpretations that gives them breadth—and that makes them appeal to differing tastes, interests, even prejudices.

A Flower Girl at a Wedding, Connecticut, 1964

Physique Contest, Venice, California, 1962

A Young Man in Curlers at Home on West 20th Street, New York, 1966

Two Female Impersonators, Club 82, New York, 1966

A Man Dancing with a Large Woman, New York, 1967

A Lady at a Masked Ball with Two Roses on Her Dress, New York, 1967

A Lady Bartender at Home with a Souvenir Dog, New Orleans, 1964

Superstar at Home, New York, 1968

A Tattooed Man at a Carnival, Maryland, 1970

Christ in an Office Building Lobby, New York, 1963

The Best of Photokina

The biggest international photography fair in the world opened in September 1972 for its regular biennial nine-day stand. The Photokina of Cologne, Germany, a combined trade show and photographic exhibition, was first held in 1950; in that year fewer than 300 exhibitors, all of them West German, displayed mostly pre-World War II photographic equipment in a space of 280,000 square feet, and the fair was visited by 75,000 local people. In 1972 some 700 exhibitors, almost half of them from countries other than Germany, mounted displays of everything from laboratory installations and photo-chemicals to microscopy instruments and astro-cameras for shooting the stars. The displays were housed in 12 halls covering 1,075,500 square feet of fair grounds. There were 250,900 visitors from all over the world.

Photokina's enormous expansion has aroused some criticism by reviewers who complain that its size has made it unmanageable and that the extravagance of its exhibits has made the show overwhelming. It has even been suggested that the picture exhibits be done away with, and that Photokina reduce itself to a trade fair. Luckily, that suggestion was not acted on in 1972, for had it been, the public would have lost the chance to view 10 unusually fine photographic exhibits—several featuring work by young photographers, in keeping with Photokina's emphasis on encouraging youth.

Pictures from two of the most intriguing shows appear on pages 48 through 59. The first show, entitled *Sequences,* was devoted to a technique that is based partly on comic strips, partly on the movies and partly on the motion studies of the pioneer photographer Eadweard Muybridge. Sequence photographs are especially popular today with photographers who find their imaginations stimulated by the opportunity to escape the confinement of the single photograph and to impose their own order on the chaotic flow of real-life events. A sequence is a series of frames that may represent a story told in sequential order, or that may describe an event—such as a man getting up from bed, walking around his room and returning to bed—that forms a circle, bringing the viewer back to the first frame. Some sequences can be viewed backward as well as forward; sometimes the subject is stationary and the camera moves around it, sometimes the opposite.

The second show was called *Women by Women.* As the Photokina catalogue somewhat archly explained, women have been a popular camera subject for men since photography was invented. How successfully men photograph women was proved by the resounding success of a 1970 Photokina show entitled *Four Masters of Erotic Photography.* In 1972, the Photokina organizers considered it appropriate to ask the subject to illustrate how she sees herself and her sisters. As demonstrated by the pictures on pages 54-58, Photokina got answers to its question that, to quote the catalogue, "were as diverse as women themselves."

GERD STERNS: *At the Photokina,* 1972

A few of the quarter-million visitors to the 1972 Photokina exhibition are silhouetted against a huge photographic enlargement of an eye. Part of a film manufacturer's display, it was almost a symbolic representation of the many-faceted aspect of the biennial cultural and technological exposition that was held in Cologne, Germany.

Pictures in Sequence

BERNARD PLOSSU: *Absence and Presence*, 1971

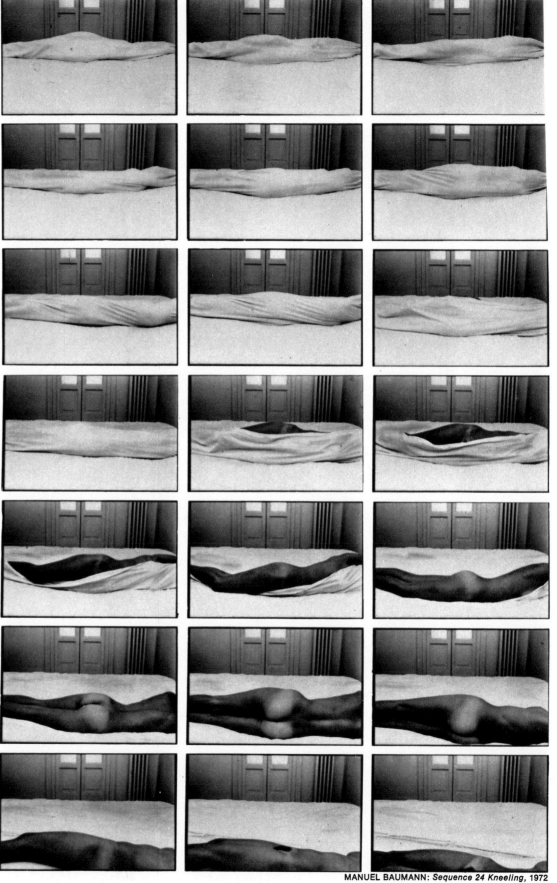

The cryptic quality of much sequence work is evident in these selections from Photokina's show. Parisian photographer Bernard Plossu says of his sequence: "It shows the different vibrations that fill a space when it is empty and when it is occupied by a human being. When empty there is no noise, smell or touch. As soon as it becomes occupied, life suddenly returns."

A 25-year-old Swiss photographer, Manuel Baumann, creates sequences that are designed to bring out an increasing contrast between a background, like the walls of an empty room, and a human body. Here he uses the technique to build up the contrast in contours and texture between his model's body, and the flat bed and the bedsheets from which she gradually unwinds.

MANUEL BAUMANN: *Sequence 24 Kneeling*, 1972

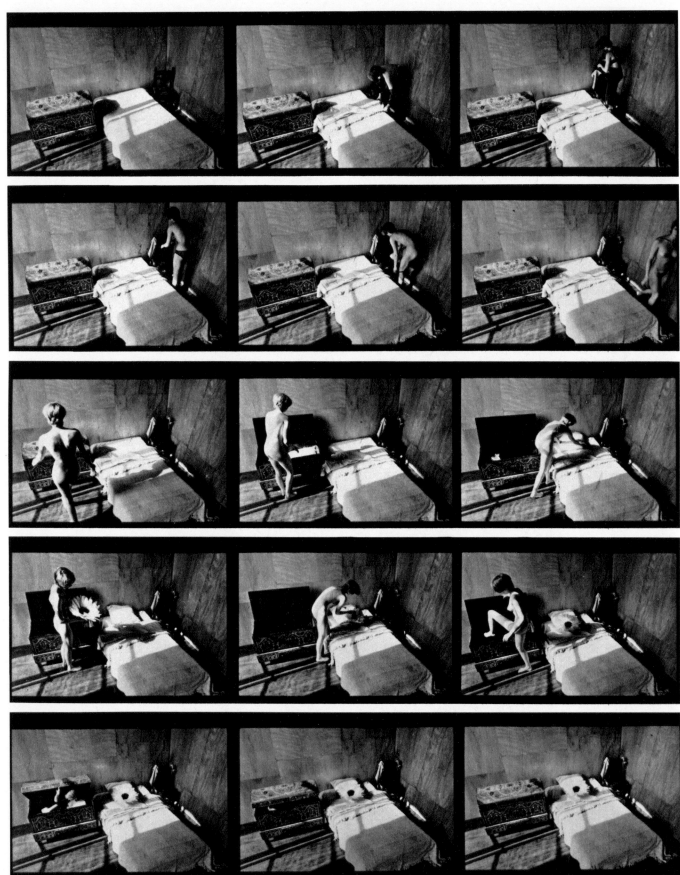

GEORGES TOURDJMAN: *Véronique Sauvage,* 1972

50

In the wry and humorous sequence at left, a girl undresses, takes a pillow and a large paper flower from her bedside chest, arranges the flower on the pillow and, having in effect tucked it in for the night, retires herself into the chest. Created by Parisian Georges Tourdjman, this sequence is reminiscent of the comic strips from which this style of photography partly derives.

The whimsically titled sequence at right, of steps leading up to a busy thoroughfare, was taken in Lucerne, Switzerland, by Jörg Diehl of that city. Diehl made each shot at eye level as he climbed the steps and then put the frames together in cinematic style so that, as the street scene emerges, the viewer feels he himself is moving up the stairs. The paradoxical twist (which Diehl intended) is that in the normal way of looking at pictures, the viewer has to read down to go up.

JÖRG DIEHL: *Visualization of a Difference in Altitude,* 1971

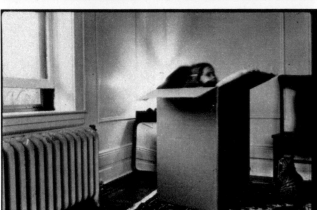 

DUANE MICHALS: *Margaret Finds a Box,* 1971

New Yorker Duane Michals, recalling a fantasy of his own childhood, shot the sequence at left, in which a little girl enters a room and finds a big, inviting box. After inspecting the box she climbs into it, closes the lid and flies away.

François Robert, a Swiss-born photographer now living in Chicago, constructed another kind of fantasy in the sequence shown at right, in which a girl appears in a mirror, dances her way across it and abruptly disappears from the viewer's sight —says Robert, "like a specter in a dream."

FRANÇOIS ROBERT: *The Girl in the Mirror,* 1970

Women by Women

In the mid-1960s, when a stripteaser named Ann Corio took her act on a tent-show circuit through the United States, women turned out to see it in such droves that they outnumbered men in the audience three to two. Miss Corio was not surprised. "Most women are frustrated stripteasers," she opined. "They like to be exhibitionists."

This frank appreciation by women of their own charms was reflected in most of the pictures submitted to Photokina by distaff photographers for the show's "Women by Women" exhibit. Of the photographers whose work was shown, an unexpectedly large number submitted nude or seminude subjects. The photographs ranged in mood from the portrait of the unselfconscious African tribeswoman by Mirella Ricciardi, at right, to the variation on the woman-as-a-sexual-temptress theme by Charlotte March, on page 58.

There were studies of the gentle dreaminess that often engulfs young girls *(opposite page)*. There were admiring photographs of women whose great natural beauty needs no adornment; and, by contrast, there were sharply candid shots of women applying liberal quantities of makeup to themselves. Pleased, if surprised, by the variety of interpretation, Photokina officials lauded the manner in which the pictures mirrored woman's love—and occasional hatred—of herself.

MIRELLA RICCIARDI: *Woman of Kenya,* **1970**

◄ *Her head proudly raised, a girl of northern Kenya's Turkana tribe shows off the rows of beads that indicate her personal wealth. Photographer Ricciardi, herself born in Nairobi, regrets what she sees as "the ever-spreading marks of Western civilization" that threaten to clothe her handsome subject, who is a member of one of the few remaining seminaked tribes in Africa.*

Her hands stained with a delicate tracery of henna —a fad borrowed from North African women—a young model turns a pensive profile to Dutch photographer Sacha van Dorsen's camera. "The clothes that fashion models have to display in their jobs often make them look horrible," says Sacha, "so I try to photograph them in a way that will bring out their natural beauty."

SACHA: *Visage*, 1970

Artful lighting catches the dramatic coiffure and ornate jewelry worn by this high-fashion model. Taken by a young German photographer whose entries celebrated the theme "Chic and Sex," the picture was one of a surprisingly small group in the exhibit that reflected the traditional female delight in wearing elegant clothes.

This intimate picture of a girl in a 1930s-type ▶ chemise was photographed through a piece of gauze that, together with the model's wistful expression, softens the picture and lends it the elements of a character study. A former Parisian model, Miss Moon has done many sympathetic portraits of weary, hard-driven mannequins.

CHRISTA PETERS: *Haute Couture*, 1971

SARAH MOON: *Untitled*, 1971

CHARLOTTE MARCH: *Belinda*, 1971

One of the show's most powerful depictions of sexual allure was this classic image of the seductive woman by German fashion photographer Charlotte March. With her long, free-blowing hair, her frank and inviting expression and her voluptuous nudity, she epitomizes the appeal women have held for men since a bewitched Adam succumbed to Eve.

The Documentary

Project Documerica 62

Twice in this century the United States government has called upon the persuasive powers of documentary photography to explain and promote far-reaching federal programs. The first venture occurred during the Great Depression of the 1930s and was concerned mainly with the plight of people. The second, begun in the spring of 1972, is concerned primarily with the condition of the environment people live in today. Both of these programs are discussed, and some of the photographs taken during the initial phase of the new program are shown on the following pages.

BILL GILLETTE: *Afternoon Sun over the Rockies*, near Loveland, Colorado

Project Documerica

If there is anything that is guaranteed to make a photographer's spirits sag, it is to be told before starting out on an assignment that the subject he is supposed to photograph is not very interesting but that everyone is counting on him to bring back some lively, dramatic pictures. That is exactly what happened to the photographers who were hired by the government's Environmental Protection Agency (EPA) in April. "Much of the subject matter is dull visual material," the agency said. "Construction of a new municipal sewage treatment plant is hardly an exciting picture possibility. But such pictures must be taken. Our waterways can only be cleaned as new plants are completed and begin to discharge almost drinkable water. Therein lies a challenge to your talent." That they responded to the challenge is clear from the results reproduced in the following pages, a selection from 47,000 photographs already shot for a project that may produce 400,000 pictures by the time it reaches completion, which is projected to be around 1980.

The EPA's idea was to document the condition of the American environment, the good as well as the bad: the unspoiled areas and the polluted air, the contaminated streams and the cluttered landscapes. The purpose was frankly propagandistic—to illustrate the environmental problems of 1972 and show what the EPA is doing to alleviate the situation, to show what people generally are doing to improve the environment, and to provide "positive pictures which speak of environmental appreciation and preservation."

The undertaking was given the name Project Documerica, and an initial task force of 46 freelance photographers was hired. It was only the second time in history that such a task force of photographers had been assembled by a government agency to document a major aspect of American life. The first big federally sponsored documentary effort was initiated during the Depression days of the 1930s. At that time Franklin D. Roosevelt's New Deal administration was making an all-out effort to prod an apathetic Congress and a largely unaware, city-dwelling public into recognizing the need for legislation to aid poor farmers. The Department of Agriculture's Farm Security Administration (FSA) hired a group of photographers to record on film the Depression victims of rural America, and the result became one of the most distinguished bodies of work in the history of American photography. For the FSA photographers produced an unforgettable array of pictures not only of the farmland that was afflicted by both drought and wind, but also of poverty-stricken sharecroppers, emaciated dust-bowl victims and indigent migrant farm workers. And the FSA project served as a launching pad for some remarkable careers, including those of such outstanding photographers as Dorothea Lange, who was famous for her pictures of migrant workers; Walker Evans of FORTUNE; Carl Mydans of LIFE; John Vachon and Arthur Rothstein of *Look;* and the renowned artist-photographer Ben Shahn.

Typical of the striking pictures taken by FSA documentarians in the 1930s, this photograph reveals the woeful aspect of an out-of-work Ohio farmer and his two sons. The photographer was Ben Shahn, a painter and graphic artist who was persuaded to take up photography in the FSA's cause and proved himself to be as expressive with a camera as he was with a brush or a pen.

In many ways the Documerica photographers were confronted with a tougher assignment. They were hired for a maximum of six weeks for any one assignment, instead of the three-year term of the FSA photographers. They were given a much broader, vaguer mandate—to document all aspects of the American environment—and the subjects they were supposed to photograph, such as sewage-treatment plants, automobile graveyards and smokestacks, were lacking in human appeal. Some of the photographers, however, were acutely aware of the human element in environmental control, and they devised ways of showing it. LeRoy Woodson Jr., assigned to document the air pollution caused by the steel mills in Birmingham, Alabama, enlisted the aid of a local organization appropriately called GASP (Greater Alliance to Stop Pollution). This organization referred him to a physician who led him to an elderly former railroad worker, a man whose lungs had been so damaged by polluted air that he constantly needs a special oxygen-producing apparatus in order to breathe *(page 72)*. Ken Heyman, covering his adopted home base of Puerto Rico, concentrated on overcrowded conditions in the slum sections of San Juan *(page 75)*.

Other photographers found the human element not only elusive but sometimes contrary. When Dennis Sipnic and an assistant stopped along a highway in Louisiana to photograph the still-clear waters of Honey Island Swamp, they were arrested and fined for obstructing traffic.

The Documerica photographers were told to use color film, although they were not bound to its use if they thought a subject demanded black and white. They were instructed to cover projects sponsored or encouraged by the EPA, but beyond that they were largely on their own. "We are going to leave the format and the nature of the coverage to each photographer," said Arthur Rothstein, the project's photographic consultant and a former member of the old FSA task force. "If he feels he can tell the story best with an 8 x 10 view camera with black-and-white film, fine. If he wants to use a 35mm camera, with color film, let him do it that way." Everybody, as it happened, elected to use 35mm cameras and color film.

The 47,000 pictures submitted by the first group of Documerica photographers have been culled, and in a year 40,000 will be filed at EPA headquarters in Washington in the world's first computerized picture library, set up to make the photographs quickly available to anyone who needs them. They are being made available to schools, the press and businesses, free of charge. In the coming years, the EPA expects to add to the file, sending photographers back to the same places to rephotograph the environment already recorded, and assigning them to cover new and emerging problems. The object, as project director Gifford Hampshire says, will be to "record what we see, whether there has been improvement in conditions or not."

CHARLES O'REAR: *Power Lines*, near Searchlight, Nevada

GENE DANIELS: *Dusting Grapevines with Sulfur*, near Fresno, California

BLAIR PITMAN: *The Steel Plant's Fumes*, Houston

MARC ST. GIL: *Junked Car Batteries' Smoke*, Houston

BLAIR PITMAN: *Rush Hour on the Southwest Freeway*, Houston

BILL SHROUT: *Cars Crushed for Recycling, Flowood, Mississippi*

DAVID HISER: *Smudge from a Garbage Dump*, Moab, Utah

CHARLES O'REAR: *Vapor Trail from a Jet,* Searchlight, Nevada

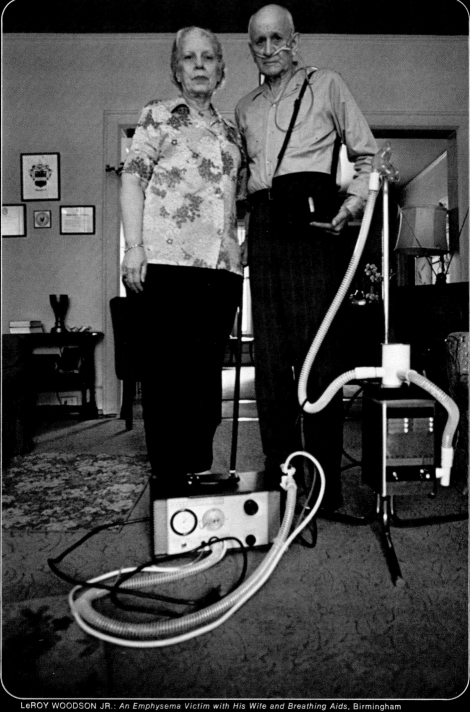

LeROY WOODSON JR.: *An Emphysema Victim with His Wife and Breathing Aids*, Birmingham

BILL GILLETTE: *Uranium Miner's Cigarette*, near Nucla, Colorado

DANNY LYON: *Second Ward*, El Paso

KEN HEYMAN: *Growing Up in Martin-Peña*, Puerto Rico

75

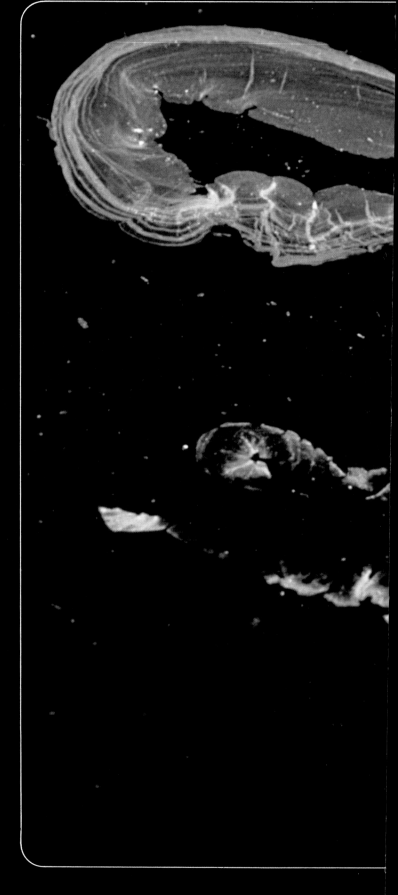

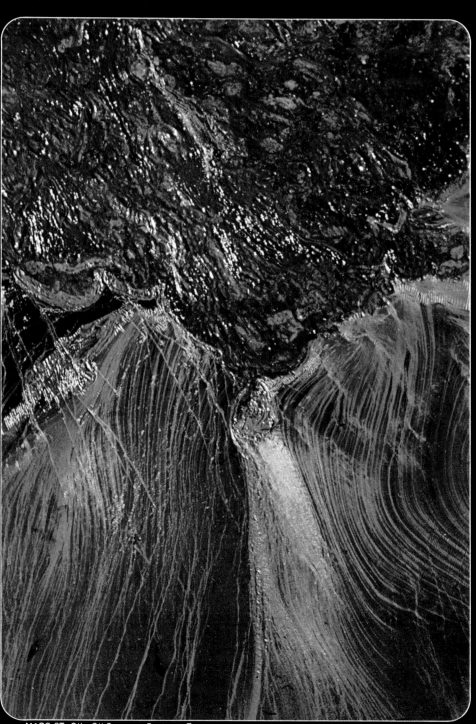

MARC ST. GIL: *Oil Seepage*, Baytown, Texas

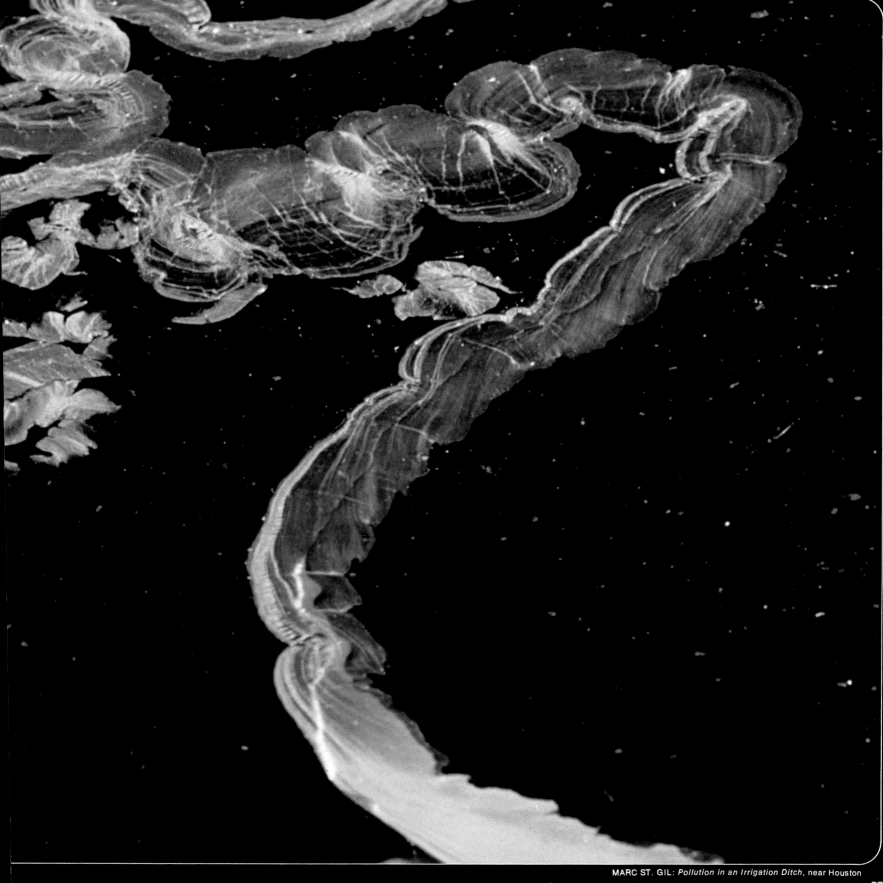

MARC ST. GIL: *Pollution in an Irrigation Ditch*, near Houston

CHARLES O'REAR: *Sunset*, Havasu Lake National Wildlife Preserve, California

The New Technology

During the past several decades most of the basic technological advances in cameras and other photographic equipment have been made in Europe and Japan. Notable exceptions were the invention of the Polaroid Land camera in Cambridge, Massachusetts, in 1948 and the development of the cartridge-loaded Kodak Instamatic camera in Rochester, New York, in 1963. In 1972 this pattern was repeated. Polaroid introduced a new instant-picture camera unlike any that it—or any other manufacturer—had ever built before. Kodak succeeded in the long-sought goal of making a practical, truly pocketable miniature camera and a high-quality film to go with it. While these cameras are intended primarily for the needs of a mass market of nonprofessional or semiprofessional photographers, they have innovative features that undoubtedly will be of interest to designers and users of more complex camera systems. What these cameras are like, and how they work, is described and illustrated on pages 82-101. At the same time there was important technological news from Germany, Japan and even from Communist China; these events are reported on pages 102-104.

In a view taken with an ultra-wide-angle lens, ▶ a technician holds the new Polaroid SX-70 Land camera in front of a massive computer control panel—one of several such computer complexes in the five new factories built to produce the camera and the film for it. This computer controls the machines that produce negative materials in the New Bedford, Massachusetts, plant.

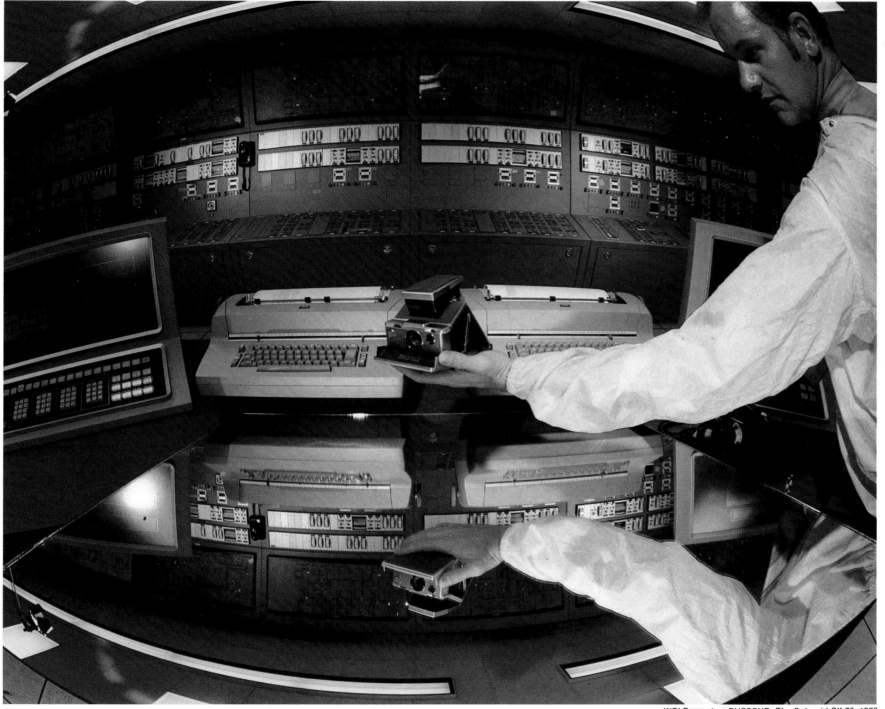

WOLF von dem BUSSCHE: *The Polaroid SX-70*, 1972

Now: One-Step Photography

For 25 years Edwin Land, the inventor of the picture-in-a-minute process, has had a private dream of the perfect camera. It would be easy to carry in pocket or purse, and there would be nothing for the photographer to do "except to compose and select the instant at which he wants to go from viewing to having. When he is happy with what he sees, the picture must appear magically outside the camera. In short, the process must be non-existent. . . ." ·

Various Polaroid Land cameras produced by his company have approached that goal, but the new SX-70, first placed on sale in November, seems to have reached it. When the owner of the new camera presses the bright red button on the front of the camera, he closes an electrical switch that sets in motion a complex and completely automated sequence of events *(pages 90-92).* A mirror rises, shutter blades open and close, a motor whirs, rollers turn and chemicals spread thinly through layers of emulsion. In 1.5 seconds a dry card with a blue-green square emerges from a slot in the camera's base, and the camera is ready for another exposure. Meanwhile the blue-green card is undergoing a metamorphosis. Quite without human intervention—there is no need to pull film out or to time development or to peel away a negative—it is changing into a brilliant color print. Land likes to call this new kind of picture taking "absolute one-step photography."

The camera in which this legerdemain takes place is technically a folding single-lens reflex. But it is unlike any SLR camera that has ever appeared before. Closed, it fits easily in a coat pocket, measuring one inch deep, four inches wide and seven inches long, and it looks like a cigar case with a periscopelike bulge on the top. At a slight pressure and upward pull on both sides of the bulge, the camera extends into open, picture-taking position. The lens comes into sight as its housing swings up from the camera base; the top part of the body rises at a 40° angle; the periscope bulge pops up to become a viewfinder, perched rather like a dormer window atop a peaked roof. It is an exceedingly odd-looking camera—and its unconventional exterior is a fair match for the unconventional array of photographic components that lie inside. In order to make the SX-70 smaller than previous Polaroid Land cameras, and to reduce the photographer's involvement in the picture-taking process, Polaroid's designers packed the camera with novel components. There is, for example, a shutter that also serves as a diaphragm—thus cutting down the space normally occupied by two separate parts. The lens is an unusually compact four-element type, and to provide the long lens-to-film distance needed to make a relatively large picture— 3⅛ x 3⅛ inches—there is a viewing-and-taking system that extends the path of the incoming light by bouncing it between a series of mirrors. Finally, there is a new color film, one that is not only self-developing but that also eliminates the unsightly negatives—an embarrassment to Land, an ardent

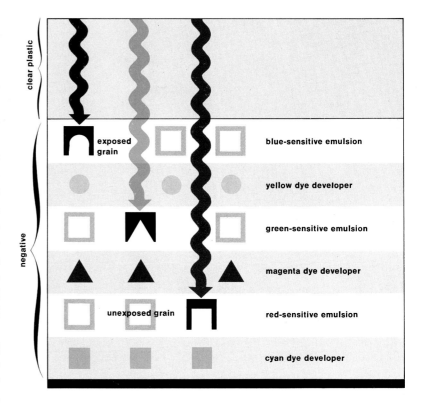

Exposing the SX-70 Negative

A color negative for the Polaroid SX-70 Land camera has three sections, each with an emulsion layer of silver halide grains (gray squares) and an adjacent layer of a dye developer. Each emulsion layer is sensitive to one primary color. When blue light strikes the top layer, blue-sensitive grains are exposed and create molecular traps (black symbols) for yellow dye in the neighboring dye developer layer. Similarly, green light creates traps in the second layer for magenta dye, and red light for cyan in the third layer. As an exposed negative is ejected, it passes between rollers that burst a pod containing an alkaline chemical, an opaque "opacifier" and white pigment, which spread to start development (right).

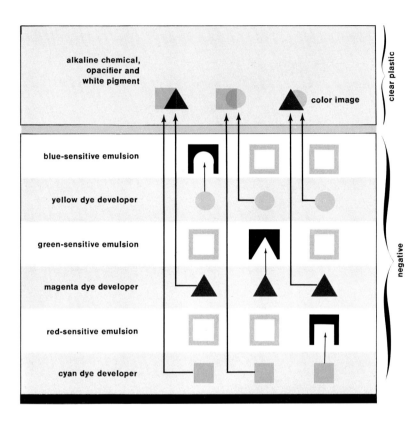

alkaline chemical, opacifier and white pigment

clear plastic

color image

blue-sensitive emulsion

yellow dye developer

green-sensitive emulsion

magenta dye developer

red-sensitive emulsion

cyan dye developer

negative

Developing the SX-70 Print

As soon as the alkaline compound spreads between the negative and print, it seeps through all layers, activating the dye developer. These molecules spread upward, and wherever one meets a silver halide trap (black symbols) it is caught. Thus the yellow dye is trapped in the blue-sensitive layer, while the magenta and cyan dyes get past that spot to reach the clear plastic where the image will form, their mixture creating the blues of the subject. Similarly, other layers trap one dye and let the others pass. When the alkaline chemical is used up, development stops, the opacifier becomes transparent, and the pigment forms a reflective base under the plastic so that only the dyes forming the image are seen.

environmentalist—that people peeled off previous Polaroid Land film and tended to drop all over the landscape.

Most of these innovations are the result of a daring design program that began with no preconceived notions of what the SX-70 should look like or contain. It was a program that pursued many solutions—some leading to dead ends, some taken for granted before they emerged—in the serene assumption that somehow the proper answers would be found.

In the design of the new film, for instance, Polaroid assumed from the start that the only way to get rid of the trash-producing negative was to leave it attached to the print and make it part of the finished picture. But to marry negative and print, Polaroid had to reverse the usual way in which its pictures were made and viewed. Instead of being printed on opaque paper, the SX-70 picture is printed on clear plastic, and it is looked at back to front, through the plastic. The necessary white background is supplied by a thin layer of white pigment that is forced between the negative and print during the development process. Viewed against this pigment, which bounces light back through the layers of colored dye, the new Polaroid image is not only exceptionally brilliant, but actually seems to have dimensional depth. The pigment also serves to mask, of course, the now-unwanted negative.

Because the new film is a self-contained unit, combining both negative and positive in one permanent package, it forms a compact 10-exposure film pack that fits neatly in the base of the camera. The film's 16 positive and negative layers are no thicker through—2/1000 inch—than the negative alone in color film used in other Polaroid Land cameras.

Along one edge of the film runs a developing pod. Contained within the pod, in precisely measured amounts, are just enough chemicals to process that particular piece of film. The chemicals include not only an alkali that starts the development process and the white pigment that provides the picture's white backing, but a third chemical—perhaps the most ingenious one of all. For a time Polaroid's designers hoped to build a darkroom for the SX-70 film within the camera body. It was to be a shallow, lightproof drawer into which the exposed film would slide for development. But the mechanics of this idea got so complicated that Polaroid decided to abandon it, and instead asked its chemists to provide a "chemical darkroom" sufficiently lightproof for the film to be developed outside the camera. This chemical darkroom is the third of the film pod's ingredients. Polaroid calls it an opacifier, but technically it is an "indicator," a substance that changes color under varying conditions of alkalinity and acidity; the chemical in the litmus paper so familiar in school chemistry laboratories is such an indicator. When the film pod is broken, the opacifier spreads between the negative and the print forming, in combination with the alkaline developing agent, an opaque blue-green coating that protects the film from light during the development process. As the image emerges and the developing agent loses its alkalinity, the indicator fades and becomes transparent.

While the film was fathered by the problem of the ecologically offensive negative, a problem raised by the film gave rise to the design of the SX-70's optics. When a viewer looks at a picture back-to-front, as he does with the new film, he is actually looking at the real scene's mirror image. But the film was so important to Polaroid, despite this flaw, that it simply taxed its optics experts to find a solution. Their answer, like fighting fire with fire, was to mirror the incoming image, so that it landed on the film in left-to-right reverse; viewed from the back through the plastic this flip-flopped image would then appear to be natural. A mirror would also solve the lens-to-film distance problem, which is peculiar to picture-in-a-minute cameras. The photographs they make cannot readily be enlarged as can negatives produced by most modern cameras; the picture must be large enough for convenient viewing, and light from the lens must travel far enough from the lens to cover the large negative area. To satisfy this requirement within a small space, a mirror helps because it "folds" the light path, making light rays travel relatively far even though the lens is fairly close to the film.

In the early stages of the camera's design, the mirror was a moving part that scanned the scene and projected it part by part, via a lens and prism arrangement, onto a moving film. It was a very sophisticated picture-making concept, and in theory it allowed Polaroid to make a full-sized print inside a very compact camera—it did not even have to be opened up for shooting. The scanning mirror, at one end of the camera, reflected the scene in small "takes" into a lens set sideways in the camera; and the lens projected the takes down the length of the camera to a moving film, where the takes were recorded. Not surprisingly, the internal complexities required to coordinate this system made it both impractical and expensive, and Polaroid decided to go to a somewhat simpler arrangement. There are four mirrors, two of them back-to-back in one double-sided unit. When the camera is open, and while the photographer is framing his picture *(page 89),* the path of the light entering the camera strikes the first of the mirrors, located on the inside of the camera's upraised cover. From that point the light bounces downward onto a second mirror, lying on top of the film pack and protecting it from exposure to light. Because this mirror has a patterned surface—rather like the ridges on the lens of a lighthouse beacon—the light returns to the first mirror on a slightly altered course, hitting it at a point different from the point of origin. From here, it bounces diagonally upward onto the third mirror. This mirror, set at an angle, beams the light directly into a magnifying lens—and finally into the eye of the viewer.

When the photographer is ready to take his picture and presses the exposure switch, this elaborately folded light path is redirected *(page 90)*. The patterned mirror, driven by a spring, swings upward on a hinge and comes to rest against the first mirror—covering the first mirror, uncovering the film and facing toward the lens a fourth, plain mirror on its undersurface. The light now enters the camera and bounces from this plain mirrored surface directly onto the film. By the time it reaches the film, however, it has traveled far enough to enlarge the image it carries to the size of the Polaroid print. In other words, by folding the incoming light, Polaroid has fitted the 4½-inch focal length needed for its 3⅛-inch-square print into a camera body only four inches high. It is the path traced by this folding light that accounts for the opened camera's distinctive triangular contours: they are in effect the light's physical embodiment.

The lens assembly that brings this light into the camera is the third of the SX-70's innovative designs. Essentially the new lens is the answer to a pack-

When a print is ejected from the SX-70 camera, no image is visible (first print, below). Instead, an "opacifier"—a bluish-green dye—covers the image as it develops, protecting it from further exposure to light. As development continues, the opacifier gradually dissipates and in about 30 seconds the image starts to become recognizable (second print). After about a minute only a trace of the opacifier is left (third print). After six minutes development is complete and all of the blue-green protective color has disappeared (fourth print), leaving the print completely visible.

aging problem: Polaroid had never before tried to fit its optics into so small a space. The designers found that, although they had a relatively compact camera when open, it was not compact enough when closed. What determined the size of the closed package was not just the lens but also its housing, together with shutter, diaphragm, light meter and other machinery. Since the housing is pushed over to lie beside the film as the camera is closed, its thickness determines the height of the closed camera and its height determines the length. To shrink this housing as much as possible required a lens unlike any normally used in cameras. It has four elements stacked so close together they make an almost solid cylinder of glass only half an inch long (most lenses of similar focal length and aperture are about twice as long). It has an unusually great focusing range, 10 inches to infinity, yet covers these distances by moving only its front element a quarter of an inch; other lenses of this focal length must generally move more than two and one half inches to cover the same range.

While the lens made a great contribution to compactness—the camera can be folded shut even with the lens fully extended—an equally important gain came from the manner in which the new camera takes care of exposure. Normally a camera controls the amount of entering light with a shutter and a diaphragm, each of which functions separately. The diaphragm is set to an opening of a particular size, and remains fixed at that size throughout the exposure, to control the amount of light entering. The shutter blades open to the full diameter of the lens instantly and remain open for a preselected time; this shutter speed controls the duration of the time light can enter to affect the film. In the SX-70, both of these functions are accomplished by the shutter; it controls both the amount of light entering and the duration of time it can enter. The shutter blades, triggered by the upward motion of the patterned mirror, open gradually, like the pupil of an eye, to form a constantly widening aperture. A tiny photocell gauges the amount of incoming light and when the aperture has opened enough so that it has admitted half the total light needed (amount combined with duration), the blades, just as gradually, close. They "know" when they have reached this halfway point through an intricate system of electronic circuitry. Preprogramed to monitor the light during a particular exposure, the circuitry adds up the incoming light energy and reverses the shutter action when the level is at midpoint. But this is not all the circuitry does. When the SX-70's 10-bulb flash attachment is inserted, the electronic system opens the shutter to a point determined by the focusing wheel, thus adjusting the opening to the subject distance, and it stays open at that point just long enough for the flash to go off, then closes.

Only a few years ago the electronics needed to perform such complicated tasks would have taken up more room than the whole camera does now. But

We at Polaroid have always felt that each person has within himself an innate potential for esthetic expression. Those of us who have been working for two decades toward a system of absolute one-step photography have felt that this potential could be realized through science, by making the picture-taking process so easy that the photographer is freed from all but artistic considerations. That is the wonderful thing about photography—you can have an inner world of science and an outer world of esthetics.

We are confident that the SX-70 system has achieved both our scientific and our esthetic goals. When we have taken the camera and film, going to the country, or to the heart of Boston, or to the rooftops in our neighborhood, we have found ourselves venturing into a delightful and rare domain we never really knew existed—like that first wonderful experience with the bicycle that suddenly stays up, a feeling of balance that we never had before. It is impossible to describe the feeling of first riding a bicycle. Similarly, no poetry for which we might grope could convey the experience of using this photographic system. There is a uniqueness to each batch of photographs brought back by each individual, easily identifiable with the personality and character of the person who took them.

I think the new camera can have an impact on the way people live. It can make a person pause in his rush through life, and in the process enrich his life at that moment. This happens as you focus through the viewfinder. It is not merely the camera you are focusing: you are focusing yourself. That is an integration of your personality, right that second. Then when you touch the button, what is inside you comes out. Photography can teach people to look, to feel, to remember in a way they didn't know they could. It is the most individualized form of creativity.

When we produced the first Polaroid camera 24 years ago we studied the kinds of pictures that people took and concluded that photography was an art, but more like a folk art than a great art. Now it seems as if the field will emerge into something other than either of these; it will be an art with a new meaning entirely. It will be a vivid manifestation of the way each individual sees the world and translates it for his own need. There can be as much variety and delight in the work of thousands of people, as much uniqueness, person by person, as we have come to expect in the past only from the greatest names in the history of art.

Edwin H. Land

the circuit board for the SX-70's automated shutter is not only amazingly small, it is just one of a collection of small electronic parts operating the picture-making process. Other electronic devices measure light, operate the diaphragm-shutter and control the motor that turns the rollers that distribute the chemicals over the exposed film. They latch and unlatch the camera's hinged mirror, and move it from taking to viewing position. They even eject, automatically, the protective black cardboard of the film pack, when the camera is loaded and the door is closed. Together with the chemical magic of the film and the ingeniously contrived optical system, they make no-fuss picturemaking very close to a reality. The work of picturemaking becomes, as Land promised, almost nonexistent for the photographer. There is, indeed, nothing for him to do but "compare and select."

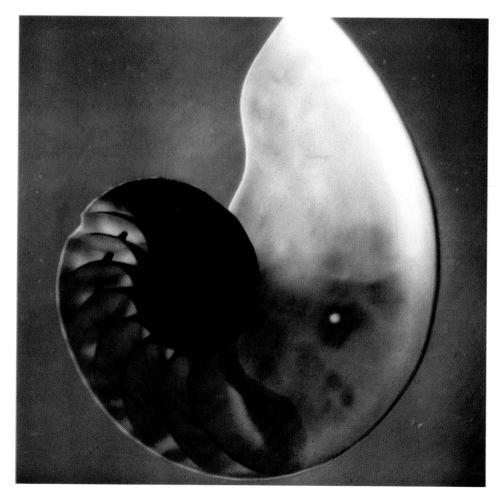

The softly translucent color seen in this chambered nautilus half shell was created by a special lighting technique that photographer Inge Reethof employed with the SX-70 camera. To produce the blue background, she used two sheets of polarizing material. One was placed on top of an illuminated square of glass and the shell was laid on the sheet. A second sheet was placed over the shell and rotated until the correct amount of light and the desired color appeared.

Viewing and Focusing

Open for picture taking, the Polaroid SX-70 Land camera points slightly downward if the base is level, as shown here. Closed (below), the camera folds to 7 x 4 x 1 inches, fitting a coat pocket. It weighs 26 ounces and sells for around $175.

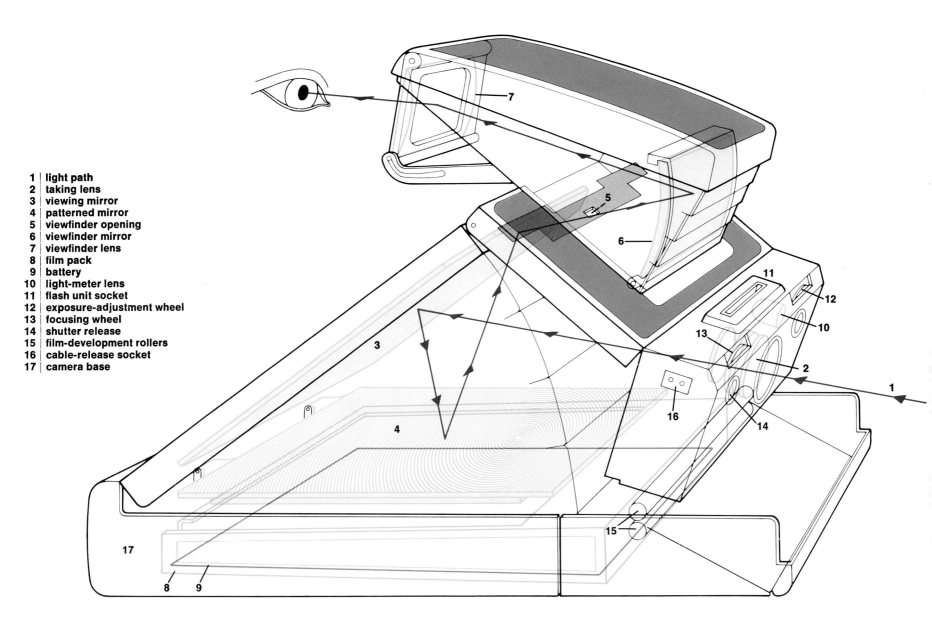

1 | light path
2 | taking lens
3 | viewing mirror
4 | patterned mirror
5 | viewfinder opening
6 | viewfinder mirror
7 | viewfinder lens
8 | film pack
9 | battery
10 | light-meter lens
11 | flash unit socket
12 | exposure-adjustment wheel
13 | focusing wheel
14 | shutter release
15 | film-development rollers
16 | cable-release socket
17 | camera base

Though technically an SLR, the SX-70 bounces light around in its innards more than familiar cameras of this general type. For viewing and focusing, light enters the camera through the taking lens (2) and is reflected downward by the viewing mirror (3). Light rays then strike the patterned mirror (4), which reflects them upward in a smaller focused beam. This beam is reflected off the viewing mirror once again and passes through the viewfinder opening (5) to strike the viewfinder mirror (6); from there it is reflected through the viewfinder lens (7) to the eye.

The SX-70 is a bellows single-lens reflex camera—but one with multiple mirrors that bounce light rays back and forth, bending the light path to extend it *(above).* The image is reflected four times before the photographer sees it, right side up, for focusing and composition. The image is reflected only once for picture taking. This allows the light path of the 4½-inch focal length to fit into a smaller package than if the image were not reflected. In addition to ten negatives, the film pack, which

slides into the base, also contains a thin, flat battery that powers both the motor and the circuitry of the camera. Since a battery is built into each film pack, a fresh power supply is available whenever the film is changed.

The camera body is made of a metal-skinned plastic in which copper, nickel and chrome are plated to a thickness of 7/1000 of an inch over a glass-filled plastic base. The resulting composite material has the strength of metal and more resiliency.

Taking the Picture

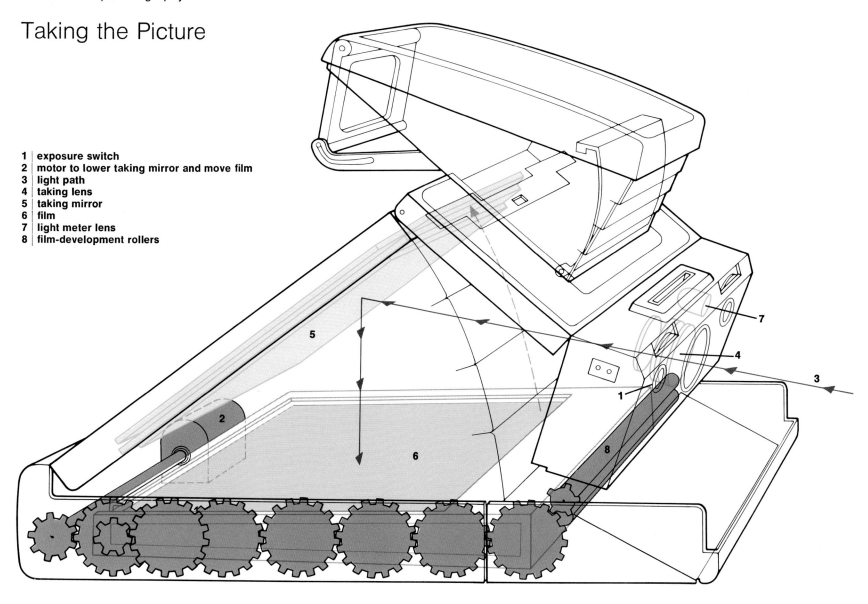

1 | exposure switch
2 | motor to lower taking mirror and move film
3 | light path
4 | taking lens
5 | taking mirror
6 | film
7 | light meter lens
8 | film-development rollers

In the SX-70 camera, the image in the viewfinder is blacked out during exposure, as in other SLR cameras. But all the other events during the moment of exposure are different. Light from the lens, instead of going directly to the film, is reflected once and then hits the film *(arrows);* in this way the light travels further inside the camera and provides a substantially larger picture.

Before the picture can be made, the shutter—which had been opened for focusing—must close so that the taking mirror can be raised into place. Only when the taking mirror is in place can the shutter begin to open to make the exposure. Assuming that there is no time exposure, the whole process takes about 3/10 second. Photographers familiar with other SLRs, in which pressing of the shutter release and making of the exposure seem instantaneous, may find the SX-70 a little disconcerting at first: it must be held steady for a fraction of a second longer than usual, or blurred pictures may result.

When the exposure switch (1) is pressed, the shutter, which was open for viewing, closes immediately and the motor (2) turns to unlatch the patterned mirror. This mirror, which is used only for viewing, then springs out of the way (vertical arrow), against the back of the camera. At this point, the taking mirror, which is on the reverse side of the patterned mirror, is in place for use. The shutter then opens to take the picture (opposite page). Light rays (3) travel through the taking lens (4) and are reflected from the taking mirror (5) down to the film sheet (6). The light meter (7) measures the light for correct exposure and the shutters close at the proper moment. The exposed film is now ready to be transported by the gear mechanism through the film-development rollers (8) and delivered to the photographer.

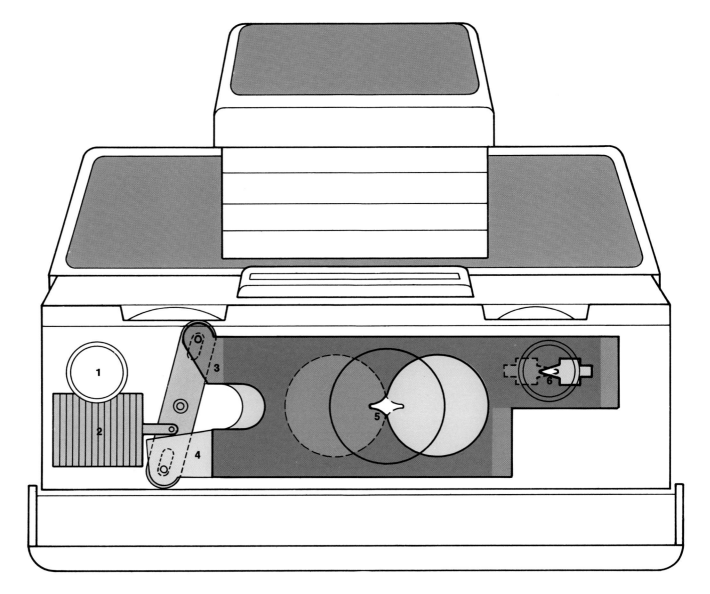

1 | exposure switch
2 | solenoid to move shutter blades
3 | front shutter blade
4 | rear shutter blade
5 | taking lens aperture
6 | light meter aperture

When the exposure switch (1) is pressed, power is supplied to a solenoid (2), an electromagnet with a moving plunger. The plunger moves a lever that slides the two shutter blades (3 and 4) past each other, closing the shutter completely. The patterned mirror flips up bringing the taking mirror into position (opposite page) and turning off the solenoid. The shutter blades then begin opening to make the exposure through the taking lens aperture (5). The light meter aperture (6) opens at the same time and the meter begins to measure incoming light. When the computer determines that half the necessary light has entered, the blades close, ending the exposure.

The shutter of the SX-70 camera has two thin metal blades, shown above in red and blue, that slide by each other when an exposure is made. Holes cut into them overlap to form two sets of holes: one, a large, round set, for the aperture of the taking lens; the other, a smaller set, for the light meter lens. When the exposure switch is pressed, the blades close in 18/1000 of a second and then, when the taking mirror is in position, start to open again. As the blades open, the light meter begins to

measure the light, sending this information to the camera's computer. The computer has been programed to allow the aperture to open until half the amount of light needed for correct exposure has passed through the lens. At this point the computer sends a signal to the solenoid to change the direction of the blades and close the aperture. The rest of the light needed to complete the exposure will thus pass through the lens in the time it takes the aperture to close completely.

The Finished Print

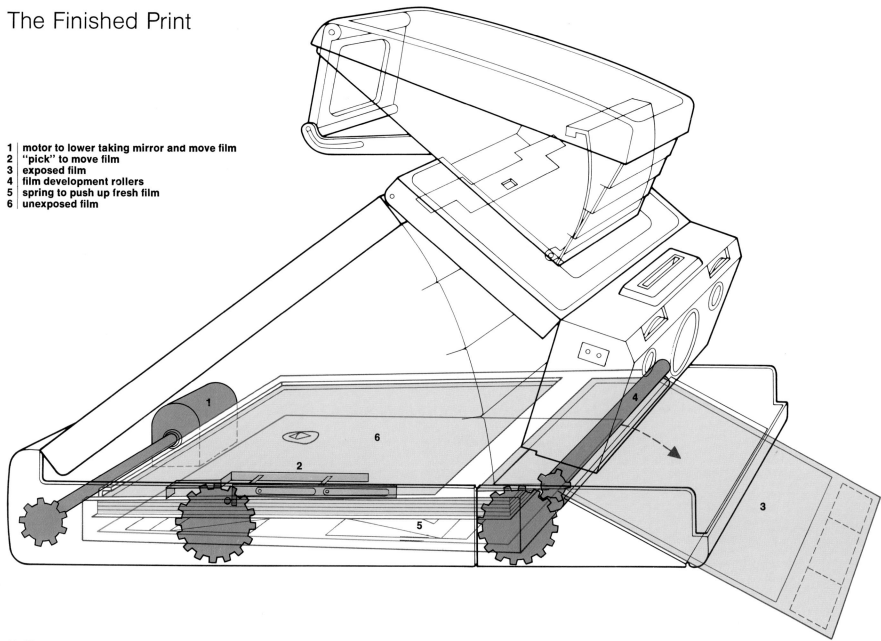

1 | motor to lower taking mirror and move film
2 | "pick" to move film
3 | exposed film
4 | film development rollers
5 | spring to push up fresh film
6 | unexposed film

Unlike other Polaroid Land cameras, the SX-70 ejects the exposed film automatically with a motor-driven gear and pick system; there is no need for the film to be pulled out by hand. Nor is there any need to count seconds and separate the negative from the print at the proper moment, for there is only enough chemical in the pod to develop the picture perfectly; when the chemical is used up, development stops automatically. By then, the opaque dye that has kept light from spoiling the process fades away, and the picture appears in color. Furthermore, there is no need to coat the prints since the clear acetate top layer provides a permanent protective cover.

On the opposite page are four color prints made by the SX-70 camera. Among them are several that demonstrate the camera's usefulness for taking extreme close-ups. The camera can focus as close as 10 inches and, by means of a slip-on auxiliary lens, life-sized images can be obtained.

When the shutter has closed after exposure, the motor (1) turns gears to move the film-pick (2) forward; the pick pulls the exposed film (3) into the rollers (4). The rollers grasp the film, break open the pod of chemicals, spreading them between the negative and positive layers of the film, and finally eject the film from the camera. As the motor rolls the film out of the camera, it also lowers the taking mirror to uncover the viewing mirror for the next exposure, and a spring (5) pushes up a fresh sheet of film from the pack (6).

Photographs taken with the SX-70 camera are ► shown actual size on the opposite page. The picture of the plate and jewelry at upper left, and those of the leaves and the cat, demonstrate the close-up capabilities of the new camera.

The Pocket Camera Breakthrough

When Eastman Kodak decided in 1968 to go ahead with the development of the Pocket Instamatic camera, it laid down one precise and unvarying requirement: the camera was not to be more than one inch thick. The process by which the company arrived at this figure was charmingly simple. It asked a group of Kodak employees to carry around in their pockets small blocks of wood about one inch thick—some a little more, some a little less—and measuring from five to six inches long and two to three inches wide. At the end of several weeks it asked these employees to comment on the comfort—or discomfort—of their small wooden packages. Almost without exception their responses indicated that while length and width were not critical factors —any unit between five and six inches long and two or three inches wide was acceptable—anything thicker than an inch was uncomfortably bulky.

Then, when Kodak introduced five models of the new Pocket Instamatic in April 1972, each camera was exactly one inch thick; the most complex model *(opposite page),* which has a rangefinder and automatic electronic controls, is 5¾ inches long and 2¼ inches wide. Each is a true shirtpocket camera, small but ready to use the instant it is pulled out, without unfolding, yet it produces big and exceptionally clear pictures. It is the quality of the prints obtained from such a tiny camera that is the breakthrough.

Making a camera so small—although it requires masterful engineering and, in this instance, ingenious use of modern materials—is not unheard of, least of all at Kodak. One of the company's most successful models was the Vest Pocket Kodak *(right),* introduced in 1915. Though somewhat wider than the present Pocket Instamatic, the Vest Pocket camera was no thicker and even slightly shorter. It was, however, a folding camera with an extendable bellows, and therefore pocketable only when closed. The bellows was needed to separate the lens far enough from the film for the camera to produce its large negative—a necessity, since a large negative was required to make an acceptable print. The problem then lay with the film, for the best route to a truly compact camera has always been to use a smaller negative. This allows shorter focal length lenses to be used and reduces the lens-to-film distance, making the camera more compact. Until now, film quality has continued to limit the practicality of very small cameras, even of the precision-made, cigarette-lighter-sized cameras currently manufactured in Europe and Japan. Their pictures, when enlarged to a practical size, are detailed enough for many purposes—including espionage, their most famous application—but they scarcely satisfy the typical photographer's demand for a clear, crisp picture and for the latest automatic controls.

Thus the development of the Pocket Instamatic had to await the development of a better film, a possibility that began to emerge sometime during the late 1960s. By that time Kodak's emulsion specialists, in the course of

"Pocket" cameras are hardly a new product for Kodak. In April 1915, the Vest Pocket Autographic Kodak, shown actual size above, was introduced. It was a folding-bellows camera that made 1⅝-x-2½-inch negatives. But the feature that made it so popular was a small door on the back that could be opened at the time of exposure to write the date and picture title on the negative. Today's Pocket Instamatic, also shown actual size at right, is an inch longer than the 1915 model. Its negatives cannot be written on—but when the prints come back from the processing laboratory, they usually have the date printed on the back.

their continuing research into the various aspects of the photographic process, had produced a color film with improved grain characteristics. The fineness of the grain resulted primarily from improvements in the dyes involved in the image-forming process; less silver compound had to be reduced to silver metal to create an image—and less silver meant less graininess. The goal was a color film that would behave as well when magnified six times as the existing Kodacolor-X did when magnified three times. This goal was reached in Kodacolor II *(pages 100-101),* the film that is the heart of the Pocket Instamatic camera.

With the problem of the film solved, a team of optical designers turned their attention to the creation of a lens to use with it. A negative so small it required at least six-times enlargement had to start with a sharp image, for which a high-grade multi-element lens would be necessary. But that lens also had to be inexpensive to produce if the camera was to suit the mass market Kodak aimed for. The obvious answer, at least for lower-priced models, was to use plastic, which can be molded dozens at a time instead of having to be ground individually, as glass lenses are. Also, plastic lenses have another advantage: they can be molded with flanges and spacing elements that make it easier to assemble the lens components quickly and accurately on a factory production line. Kodak had used plastic before but never for a lens requiring such sharpness. Consequently, when its designers produced a prototype—a three-element lens of acrylic plastic—Kodak put the new system to a severe test. It mounted the lens in a high-quality 35mm camera, loaded the camera with the new color film in a 35mm size, then blocked off a small section of the exposed negative—a section that was approximately the size of the Pocket Instamatic's picture area—and enlarged that section about six times. If the enlargement from this test matched the picture quality of a color print from a standard Instamatic, the new lens and film combination could be judged a success. It was.

Having developed a film and a lens to match it, Kodak now faced the problem of producing a package for them—a package that would contain within a very small interior space all the picture-taking conveniences to which camera owners have become accustomed. It was at this juncture that the blocks of wood were passed around and the size and shape of the camera were determined. A new problem immediately arose, one that is encountered in designing any camera and is particularly difficult to solve in an inexpensive subminiature camera. This is the necessity of keeping the lens-to-film distance consistently accurate. The problem can be solved in two parts. The first is to guarantee that every time a roll of film is placed in the camera, the film will lie flat in the film plane. The second is to ensure that the lens in each camera is the correct distance from the film.

Because Kodak wanted to keep the convenience of a cartridge loading camera, positioning the film accurately meant designing a new cartridge. It forms, with the back of the camera, a film channel and pressure plate arrangement similar to that used in expensive 35mm cameras. It keeps the film remarkably flat and positions it accurately in the film plane each time a cartridge is inserted into the camera. To solve the second part of the problem —setting the lens at precisely the correct distance from the film—a drastic change in manufacturing methods was necessary. The only way to position the lens accurately enough in the new camera was to adjust each lens assembly individually. As the lens reaches one station on the production line it is combined with another part that determines the final lens-to-film distance, and the position of the lens within this part is measured electronically. If the position is off by as much as 1/1000 inch, a needle swings on a dial to register the error—and a worker screws the lens in or out to adjust its position until the dial records an accurate setting.

Besides the problems created by the film size and the degree of magnification, the designers and engineers had trouble fitting their ideas into such a small scale. To help them over this discouraging psychological hurdle, the chief of the design team set up a permanent exhibit. He took apart a fine watch, arranged its minuscule parts on a piece of black velvet, and placed a binocular microscope nearby for viewing them. Whenever a member of the team became discouraged with the problems of miniaturization, he could step up and study the watch parts, and be reassured.

New feats of miniaturization were indeed necessary. For instance, the camera requires a large number of tiny metal gears and levers. Ordinarily such parts are machined from solid metal, a process that is both time consuming and costly. But there is a modern way to make precision parts by molding them from finely powdered metal. The powdered metal is pressed into a shape, much as aspirin is pressed into tablets, and then heated until the metal particles fuse solid. Unfortunately, however, the manufacturers who used the technique were unwilling to meet the specifications for parts so small; in fact, they said that it could not be done. So Kodak went into the powdered-metal business and made its own pressed-metal parts—some of them half the thickness of any previously produced by the process.

A similar feat was performed with plastics. At first experts did not believe plastic parts could be made as thin—and yet as strong—as those needed by the camera. But they eventually succeeded in molding parts so thin— 10/1000 inch thick—that they are rightly referred to as "flashes" of plastic.

These problems with film flatness, lens placement and miniaturized parts were shared by all five models (which range in price from about $30 to $130). But the more expensive models had special miniaturization problems of their

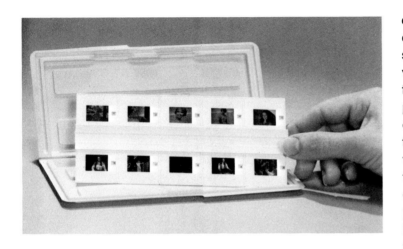

Color slides produced by the Kodak Pocket Instamatic are returned to the photographer in 1⅜-inch-square plastic mounts, which are clipped to a plastic "stick" in groups of 10, as shown above. A full roll of 20 exposures can thus be contained on two sticks, which are packaged in a thin wallet that protects the slides.

own. Built into them are such conveniences as electronic devices and circuits that measure the available light and automatically control shutter speed. And in the most expensive model there are also a rangefinder and devices for automatically controlling the size of the aperture. In order to fit all this electronic gear into a cavity slightly more spacious than the inside of a pack of king-sized cigarettes, the designers shrank every component. The exposure information collected by the light meter is evaluated by three integrated circuits, each the size of the tip of a little finger; together they do the work of 50 transistors. The pea-sized motor that controls the aperture and the equally small electromagnet that operates the shutter are wrapped with copper wires, some of which are only 14/10,000 inch in diameter. The battery pack, encased in bright yellow or red plastic, looks like something from a box of Cracker Jack and weighs half an ounce, while the circuitry connecting the various electronic components is printed on flat, flexible ribbon that wraps and bends its way around objects with far more facility than wires and also behaves more reliably.

But successful miniaturization raised new problems that had nothing to do with machinery. One of these was dirt. A dust particle on a negative only 13mm by 17mm can blot out an entire area of the picture. Dealing with this drawback required a new system of film handling. The negatives are returned from the developer in strips, each strip encased in plastic so the photographer need never touch the negatives themselves. Similarly, when he orders color transparencies, the slides are returned framed and sealed in plastic *(left),* ready for showing in the pocket-sized projector designed especially for them.

A new camera, a new film, new film-handling aids and a new projector —even a new array of film-processing machines for the commercial photofinisher—all this adds up to a completely new system of photography. The subminiature camera, after years of being considered simply a novelty, may finally have come into its own. And perhaps more important, the developments that made the Pocket Instamatic possible promise further progress in miniaturization—and greater convenience—for cameras intended for professional and semiprofessional work.

The Model 60 Exploded

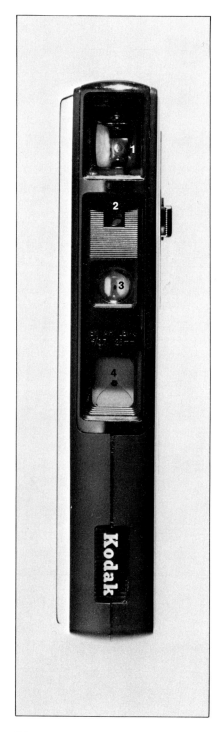

A Kodak Pocket Instamatic camera Model 60, seen from the front at far left, is shown broken down into its major sections. The first section at left is the top plate; the second the housing for electrical and optical parts of the camera; the third section includes the lens, light meter and flash-cube socket, as well as a motor, an electromagnet and the circuitry to control them. The fourth section is the mechanical heart of the camera, including the gears for advancing the film and rotating the flash cube. Such miniature machinery makes excellent photographs because of improved film, which gives sharp prints *(following pages)* from a negative only 13mm x 17mm in size.

1	viewfinder
2	rangefinder
3	light meter
4	taking lens
5	top plate
6	opening for viewfinder
7	opening for light meter
8	opening for taking lens
9	distance scale (metric)
10	distance scale (feet)
11	focus control
12	connection for wiring to shutter release
13	shutter release
14	light meter
15	taking lens and housing
16	flash-cube socket
17	motor to set diaphragm
18	electromagnet to control shutter
19	ribbon electrical circuitry
20	film-advance mechanism
21	viewfinder-rangefinder and housing
22	eyepiece
23	battery
24	film-loading door
25	film cartridge
26	bottom plate

The New Film

Kodacolor II, the new color print film made especially for the Kodak Pocket Instamatic cameras, has a finer grain and therefore is sharper than Kodacolor-X, the film used in older Instamatics. A comparison of negatives and prints from both films makes clear that although the newer film *(bottom)* is magnified twice as much as the older film to give a standard print, both prints appear equally clear and sharp with good contrast and color values.

Both sets of negatives on this page were taken at the same distance from the subjects. The subjects in the Kodacolor-X pictures are smaller because the lens in the older Instamatic has a shorter focal length in proportion to its negative size. This produces a wider angle of view and therefore makes everything in the pictures appear smaller.

On the opposite page small sections from both films have each been enlarged 80 times. These examples make even clearer the fact that Kodacolor II is a superior film.

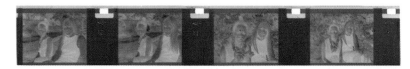

Earlier models of Kodak Instamatic cameras use 126-size film, which produces a negative about 1⅛ inches square (upper strip). The standard print from this negative is about 3½ inches square, a magnification of three times the size of the negative. The new Pocket Instamatic cameras use 110 film, which gives a rectangular negative about 1/2 x 11/16 inches (lower strip). The standard print from this negative (bottom) is about 3½ x 4½ inches, a magnification of six times the negative size. The 110 film produces an excellent print even though it is magnified twice as much as 126 film.

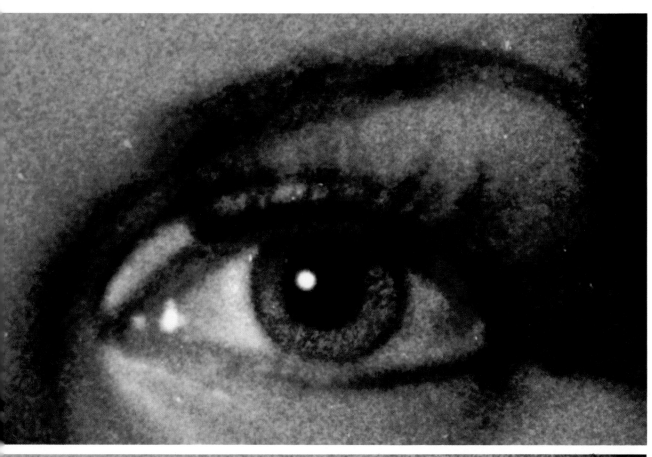

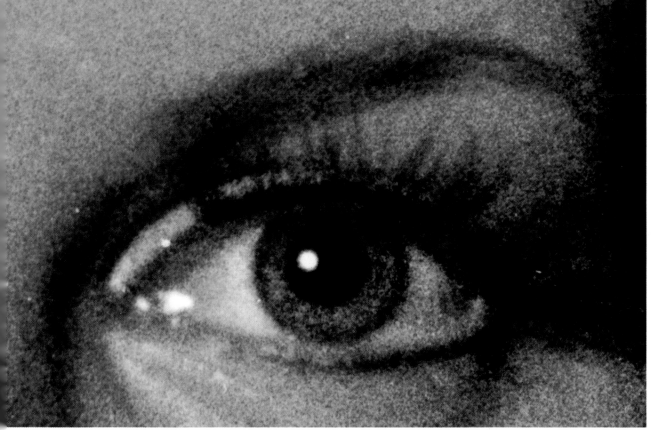

The two details on this page provide a striking demonstration of the sharpness of the new Kodacolor II film. The top picture is a section of a print from a Kodacolor-X negative, the bottom picture one from a Kodacolor II negative; both are enlarged 80 times. The Kodacolor II print is clearly sharper. The clumps of dye are smaller and harder edged, making details more distinct. This can be seen more easily if the page is held at arm's length—about 3 feet away. The eyebrows are more sharply defined in the bottom picture, as is the line between the iris and pupil of the eye.

Other Cameras and Equipment

Automatic Shutter Controls

A major step in automating professional picture taking made its official debut at the Photokina exposition in Cologne in October: film exposure adjustment with shutter speeds automatically set by a through-the-lens metering device. This technique of automatic exposure regulation permits the photographer to choose his aperture, and thus select the depth of field he will get—a control over picture quality that was not readily provided by earlier cameras that have automatic exposure determination, in which the meter set the aperture rather than the shutter speed.

Production models of several new automatic-shutter SLRs were shown at Photokina: among them, the Pentax Electro Spotmatic (or ES), the Yashica AX, the Nikkormat EL and a model from Minolta. A prototype of the Pentax ES was shown earlier in 1972.

To use these cameras the photographer first sets the desired aperture. The light meter sends its measurement to a built-in computer, which then sets the shutter speed for correct exposure. An additional piece of sophisticated circuitry is needed in this type of camera —a memory device that can hold the shutter speed measurement while the light meter blacks out as the mirror swings up during exposure. Cameras of this type have "electronically controlled" shutters, since the actual shutter is the traditional mechanical device powered by a spring, but under the computer's control. Many of the new cameras have manual controls to allow the photographer to override the automatic shutter-setting device.

German-Japanese Collaboration

A new pattern of international partnerships among photographic manufacturers was reinforced in June with the announcement of a cooperation agreement between Ernst Leitz of Wetzlar (makers of the Leica) and the Japanese firm of Minolta. The two companies agreed to trade technical personnel and knowledge and to share production facilities for making camera accessories and optical equipment. Eventually they will share patents, and, although all details of the agreement have not yet been spelled out, they do not rule out more extensive cooperation, nor the possibility of a Leitz-Minolta camera in the future. As a beginning, each company will, by early 1973, have two lenses on the market that can be fitted to the other's camera.

In joining efforts, Leitz and Minolta followed the lead set a few months earlier by Zeiss Ikon-Voigtländer of West Germany, one of the world's oldest and most respected manufacturers of pho-

Asahi Pentax ES

Yashica AX

tographic equipment. Zeiss had joined Asahi of Tokyo (makers of the Pentax) for the manufacture and distribution in Japan of eyeglasses and microscope lenses—after announcing that it was phasing out its amateur camera production although it would still manufacture Contarex and Hologon cameras. Also looking eastward was Rollei of West Germany, which transferred some of its production to Singapore in 1972. Rollei has also completed an agreement with Zeiss to manufacture lenses under the Zeiss name in Singapore. These globe-girdling ties were made necessary at least in part by high costs in West Germany; in some instances, labor rates in the Orient are only an eighth of those in Europe.

High-Speed Motorized Camera
A motor-driven 35mm camera that can take 8 to 10 photographs per second —twice the rate possible with other sequence cameras—was tested at the Winter Olympics in Sapporo, Japan, in February and shown at the Photokina fair in Cologne in September. Eight frames—about one second's filming —of the Japanese skier Y. Fukuhara making a downhill run during a competition in spring 1972 are shown below.

The new Canon High-Speed Motor Drive F-1 SLR can operate faster because it is the first to combine motor drive with a pellicle mirror—an ultra-thin, half-silvered viewing mirror that remains fixed instead of swinging out of the light path for each exposure. Most of the light coming through the lens reaches the film to make the exposure, but enough is reflected up into the eyepiece for viewing and focusing.

Since the mirror does not have to move up and down with each exposure, the speed of repeated shots can be substantially increased. In addition, the image seen in the viewfinder is never blacked out, so the photographer can keep a moving subject continuously in view. The camera, which costs around $1,000, is intended for news and sports photographers and is available only on special order.

A Compact SLR
A new 35mm single-lens reflex camera shown at the Photokina exposition in Cologne in September is smaller, lighter and quieter than most other SLRs—its shutter and mirror noise have been reduced by almost half from previous levels by means of a special air damper and more than 20 Olympus-developed shock absorbers; with its standard f/1.8 lens, it measures a mere 5⅜ x 3¼ x 3⅕ inches, and it weighs just 23.3 ounces. As only one part of a complete new system presented in 1972 by Olympus of Japan, the M-1 camera can be fitted with 30 interchangeable lenses, from an 8mm fisheye to a 1000mm telephoto. It also has some 250 other accessories that have been designed for it exclusively, including a motor film drive, a 250-exposure magazine, five special macro lenses designed especially for close-up work and a complete range of standard accessories.

Versatile Automatic Flash
Several new pieces of electronic flash equipment introduced by Honeywell in 1972 add versatility to units that auto-

Canon High-Speed Motor Drive F-1 Camera

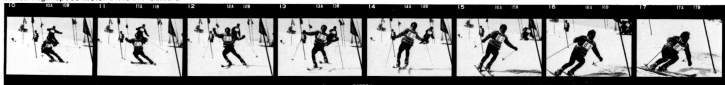

HIROSHI YOKOYAMA: *Skier in Slalom Race,* Japan, 1972

matically regulate flash duration to give correct exposure. Five new units permit control over depth of field by allowing the photographer a choice of up to four f-stops at a single film speed; earlier types could be used only at one f-stop for each combination of subject distance and film speed. In addition, some of these units, if used with a small accessory or with a special camera, do not have to be attached to the camera itself or pointed directly at the subject, but may be placed in any position on or off camera and at the same time retain automatic exposure control.

This multiposition automatic flash was made possible by separating the light-control device from the rest of the unit. This device was made available as an independent attachment, called the Honeywell Strobo-Eye Sensor, that fits most camera accessory shoes; it measures light reflected by the subject,

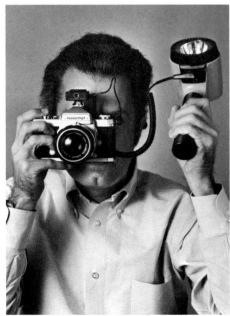

Honeywell 772 with Strobo-Eye Sensor

calculates the flash duration needed and signals the flash unit accordingly. The flash unit can thus be set on the camera or at any distance away from the camera for direct lighting, or held at an angle for bounce lighting as shown in the picture at left below. The flash unit is connected to the sensor by a standard synchronization cord. (A new model of the Pentax Spotmatic camera, the IIa, has the Strobo-Eye unit built into the camera body itself.)

The Strobo-Eye Sensor is an extra accessory for use with three of the new variable-aperture automatic flash units, models 462, 772 and 882. The 462 is a small unit that can illuminate objects 2 to 28 feet distant. The 772 and 882, which differ in their batteries, cover 2 to 40 feet, with a range of four f-stops each when used with the Strobo-Eye, and provide another useful feature: a green signal light that indicates whether sufficient light can reach the subject for proper exposure. To use this test arrangement, a trial exposure can be made by placing the flash unit and camera in the desired positions and then pressing the open-flash button on the unit. If enough illumination has reached the subject, the green light pops on.

The other two variable-aperture-unit models are simpler. They do not have the green-light tester, are not designed for use with the remote sensor, and must be mounted on the camera and aimed directly at the subject. Both units, however, give the photographer a choice of three f-stops. With the model 360, for example, f/2, f/2.8 or f/4 may be used with a film speed of ASA 25. A calculator dial conveniently located on the back of this unit is set at the correct ASA and the usable f-stop range is read

off the dial. The control unit measures the light reflected from the subject automatically and times the flash duration for correct exposure.

New Cameras from China

In an ironic turnabout of history, the Japanese, who started out to become the world's No. 1 camera makers by imitating German designs now find their method being copied by the Chinese. Five cameras from behind the bamboo curtain appeared in U.S. photographic supply houses in 1972, and while some of the models resemble German types of the 1950s others recall Japanese cameras of 15 to 20 years ago.

The Seagull 203 is a 2¼ x 2¼ folding-bellows-type camera with rangefinder focusing, similar in design to the Zeiss Super Ikonta fondly remembered by many photographers. The Seagull 4A and Pearl River 4 are both 2¼ x 2¼ twin-lens reflexes modeled after the Rollei-

The Seagull 203

flex. Also available is a compact 35mm rangefinder camera, the Seagull 205, and the Seagull DF, a full-sized 35mm SLR camera. Since all of these cameras lack such up-to-date features as built-in light meters, they are relatively inexpensive; all of them cost less than $100.

In the career of every good photographer there is always a moment just before he gains widespread notice. His work has been recognized by a few influential people in the photographic community but he is not yet known to the general public. He is a "new photographer," and one of the things a photography yearbook should do is find and introduce him and his fellows to a wider audience. To help identify the major new photographers of 1972, PHOTOGRAPHY YEAR called on a group of outside experts, who nominated a total of 48 men and women as worthy of attention (page 109). All were asked to submit portfolios of their work in time for it to be considered for publication in this edition of PHOTOGRAPHY YEAR, and 43 of those nominated did so. From the several thousand prints, transparencies and photographic constructions they sent in, the Editors made the final selection of the four photographers whose work appears on pages 110-142.

JUDY DATER

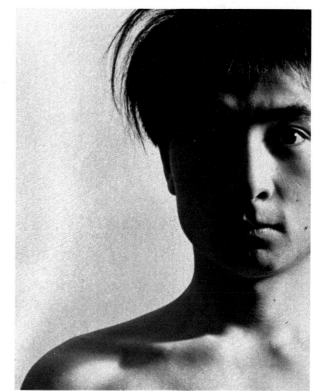

YASUHIRO IHARA

CARL TOTH

JOHN BANASIAK

A Search for New Photographers

Though each of the four photographers whose work is shown on the following pages has a strongly individual way of working, together they are broadly representative of contemporary attitudes and trends. In addition, all of them have reached a point in their careers that is exciting not just to the photographers themselves, but also to editors, curators, teachers and perhaps to small groups of gallerygoers or fellow artists who have become aware of their work. At this point they are on the threshold of a wider recognition by the general public.

Judy Dater *(pages 110-117)* is a portraitist who uses traditional approaches to photograph some very untraditional people. She is a California housewife and teacher. Carl Toth *(pages 126-133)* makes highly personal experiments in form and color. Yasuhiro Ihara *(pages 118-125)* came to the United States from his native Japan in 1969; he is a storyteller whose spare and elegant images recall the great masters of Japanese printmaking. John Banasiak *(pages 134-142)* worked as a part-time bartender while studying photography, and his pictures taken on the job combine the artlessness of the snapshot with a warm feeling for ordinary people. At 22 he is the youngest of the four new photographers whose work is included.

These four were chosen from a list proposed by a panel of six distinguished specialists *(opposite page).* The experts included a wide range of workers in the field: teachers, curators, editors and critics, as well as photographers. Geographically they were spread from California to Switzerland. In considering new photographers there were no restrictions of age, race or sex, and every individual style of work was welcomed. However, the consultants were asked to exclude from consideration photographers who had already reached the point of making a living from their artistic work alone. Also excluded were those whose work had already received widespread attention—in their own books, in major museum shows or as significant parts of museum collections. The final selection was made on the basis of sample work sent in by 43 of the 48 nominees. The aim of the Editors was to find photographers so new that they were unknown even to experts only a few months ago. But the final criteria were solid achievement and excellence that deserved—but had not yet gained—wide public recognition.

The PHOTOGRAPHY YEAR
Panel of Consultants

PETER BUNNELL
McAlpin Professor of the History of Photography
and Modern Art, Princeton University; former
Curator of Photography, The Museum of Modern
Art, New York

ROBERT HEINECKEN
Photographer and Associate Professor of Art,
University of California at Los Angeles

MARK KAUFFMAN
Photography Editor, *Playboy* magazine, Chicago

ALLAN PORTER
Editor, *Camera* magazine, Lucerne, Switzerland

AARON SISKIND
Adjunct Professor of Photography, Rhode Island
School of Design, Providence

DAVID VESTAL
Photography Critic and Visiting Artist, School of
the Art Institute of Chicago

Photographers Nominated by the Consultants

RONNA BAKER, *Chicago*
LEWIS BALTZ, *Venice, California*
*JOHN BANASIAK, *Harvey, Illinois*
MICHAEL BECOTTE, *Rochester, New York*
RON BENVENISTI, *New York City*
MICHAEL BISHOP, *San Francisco*
BARBARA BLONDEAU, *Philadelphia*
ELLEN BROOKS, *Los Angeles*
ANITA CHERNEWSKI, *New York City*
MARK COHEN, *Wilkes-Barre, Pennsylvania*
LINDA CONNOR, *San Francisco*
PIERRE CORDIER, *La Hulpe, Belgium*
*JUDY DATER, *San Anselmo, California*
MICHAEL deCOURCY, *Vancouver*
JONAS DOVYDENAS, *Chicago*
WILLIAM EGGLESTON, *Memphis*
LEN GITTLEMAN, *Watertown, Massachusetts*
ROBERT HARMON, *Harrison, New York*
*YASUHIRO IHARA, *New York City*
JOSEPH JACHNA, *Oak Lawn, Illinois*
KEN JOSEPHSON, *Chicago*
PETER KAPLAN, *New York City*
WARREN KRUPSAW, *Reston, Virginia*
PAUL KWILECKI SR., *Bainbridge, Georgia*
BILL LARSON, *Philadelphia*
ADAL MALDONADO, *San Francisco*
LEE MARSHALL, *New York City*
ROGER MERTIN, *Rochester, New York*
RAY METZKER, *Philadelphia*
OZIER MUHAMMED, *Chicago*
BEA NETTLES, *Philadelphia*
BART PARKER, *Narragansett, Rhode Island*
TOM PORETT, *Thunder Bay, Ontario*
ROBERT RANSOM, *Oshkosh, Wisconsin*
JACQUES RICHEZ, *Rhode St. Genese, Belgium*
RON ROSENSTOCK, *Worcester, Massachusetts*
EVA RUBENSTEIN, *New York City*
STEVE SALMIERI, *New York City*
STEPHEN SHORE, *New York City*
LAURENCE SIEGEL, *New York City*
KEITH SMITH, *Beaufort, South Carolina*
MICHAEL STONE, *Ellensberg, Washington*
CHARLES SWEDLUND, *Cobden, Illinois*
VAL TELBERG, *Sag Harbor, New York*
*CARL TOTH, *Bratenahl, Ohio*
ALWYN SCOTT TURNER, *New Orleans*
CHRISTIAN VOGT, *Basel, Switzerland*
JOHN WOOD, *Alfred, New York*

Work of these photographers is shown on the following pages.

Judy Dater: The Feminine Eye

Judy Dater is not the first woman photographer to photograph women, but she may well be the first to convey the peculiar atmosphere of pride, animation and intransigence that surrounds the liberated young women of today. She photographs artists, actresses, models, dancers. They are self-possessed—even self-absorbed—and ruled by difficult occupations and by the need they have to impose themselves on the world. Often they are hauntingly beautiful, and even when they are  not, they seem to exude a demanding vitality. They are never coy, never consciously seductive, never submissive and, if they take off their clothes, they do so simply to make themselves comfortable, without thinking of how it will look to others or of what attention their nudity may attract.

They live, in short, in a world where old rules are flouted and the traditionally separate roles of man and woman do not exist. Often, indeed, they seem to belong to an uncompromisingly Amazonian society, but one that is strangely theatrical. The women are always in costume, never in the kind of clothes ordinary women buy in department stores, and sometimes their clenched hands and fixed stares suggest a dramatic intensity of feeling.

Most of Dater's pictures are portraits, carefully posed and lighted in the style that leading photographers at the turn of the century adapted from paintings by old masters. She acknowledges her debt to such distinguished photographers of that period as Gertrude Käsebier, a successful New York portraitist; part of Dater's power stems from the contrast between the old-fashioned formality of her approach and the up-to-dateness of her feeling.

Most of her sitters are friends, but it would be hard to deduce her life from her unconventional pictures. Aged 31, she is married to Jack Welpott, himself a distinguished photographer, who first got her interested in the art. She studied photography in California, where she now lives and teaches.

"She is a free soul, the epitome of the liberated ▶ young woman," says Judy Dater of the painter friend who posed for this picture; and so she seems to be. Sitting with a cigarette in her own backyard, she has taken her shirt off, just as a man might do on a warm day, and seems to be saying, "Why not?" Like most of Dater's portraits, this one was taken with a 4 x 5 view camera.

Maggi Frish, Painter, 1970

Model and Dog, 1969

◀ *Dater was posing a model when a dog looked in at the door, and she snapped this informal shot with her 2¼ x 2¼ twin-lens reflex camera. She says that neither dog nor model was aware of the other's presence. However, a female critic who saw the photograph thought the dog was menacing the woman, while a male interpreter felt that the woman was rejecting the dog.*

In this picture, the photographer says she was chiefly interested in the play between the dark and light shapes of the seated model, the chair and the background. But the viewer, perhaps disturbed by the sexual ambiguity, asks: "Is it a boy or a girl?" At first glance it could be either, but a closer look at the picture reveals the free soul whose portrait appears on page 111.

Maggi Frish, Painter, 1970

Antique clothes and soft lighting give this study of a young mother and child an old-fashioned look. However, there is not a remnant of old-fashioned sentiment in it. The mother gazes calmly, even coldly, at her child. The child, meanwhile, is completely absorbed in playing with a rattle that blurs her hand, her head and even the glittering metal cross on her mother's breast.

Kathleen and China, 1972

As unsentimental as the picture on the opposite
page is this portrait of a young Puerto Rican
mother and her child. The mother, who
was described by the photographer as "a
contemporary gypsy," gazes out distrustfully at
the world. With a protective gesture, she pulls the
child to her, and the strength of their defiance is
heightened by the drama of the lighting.

Maria and Legend, 1970

More than most portraits, this one suggests a story. But its meaning remains unfathomable, and the photographer declines to explain. The girl seems dressed for bed, yet she is out of doors crouching at the foot of a tree, clutching her knee and the gnarled wood behind her till her tendons are visible. She stares out with an expression of fright, or desire, or perhaps the urge to kill.

Twinka, 1970

This sitter, with her benign smile and calmly joined hands, is possessed by an almost preternatural calm, as if she had already seen all that the world had to offer and had overcome any temptation to become involved. The contrasting floral patterns of chair and dressing gown obviously attracted Dater's attention, and add a decorative note to a study of human character.

Suzan Remy, 1972

Yasuhiro Ihara: The Traveler

The reaction of a stranger arriving in the big city is the idea that Yasuhiro Ihara chose to convey with his photographs. And "idea" is the key word for understanding his work. For Ihara, though a photographer, is a believer in the ancient Oriental concept of art as a contemplative activity. Traditionally, Chinese and Japanese painters went out to the country to contemplate a mountain or a spray of cherry blossoms, then returned to their houses to paint, not just the appearance, but the inner-

most essence of what they had seen. In the same way, Ihara roams the streets of New York, taking in the strangeness of a big city. He keeps a small notebook in which he occasionally jots down descriptions or locations he likes, and then when his idea comes he refers to these notes and returns to the locations to make photographs.

To Ihara the means of expressing his ideas are secondary. He came to photography after years of studying art in Tokyo and New York, and he does not care much about the technical side of the medium. What is important to him is being able to record an image so that it conveys his reactions to it.

In the following pages he has recaptured the special feeling he had himself when he arrived in New York—loneliness, curiosity, an occasional sense of shock. He used locations in and near New York City ranging from Kennedy airport to the Staten Island ferry, and he got a Japanese friend to serve as a stand-in for himself.

Many other newcomers to New York may recognize their own feelings and responses in these evocative pictures. But the city Ihara records—so spare and modern—could as easily be Milan or São Paulo as New York. Similarly, the bare design of his pictures makes them unspecific and thus universal. In their elegant simplicity they recall the work of the great Japanese printmakers and the delicately allusive Japanese poetry known as haiku.

The Arrival

Joy

Meditation

121

The Up Staircase

Mirror of the Sky

A Moment Seized

Farewell

Carl Toth: Fractured Perspectives

In his photographs Carl Toth has tried to break out of conventional ways of making pictures. There is no reason, he feels, why a photographer must be restricted to one view of a subject. To avoid this limitation Toth may move around a subject and shoot it from different sides or, standing still, take several different views from one place. There is also no reason still photography should not show motion, so Toth sometimes shifts his camera while shooting, or photographs moving objects. Finally, he feels that there is no reason a photograph must consist of a single frame with four sides, so he combines several frames to make more complex pictures that may have as many as 17 sides. The results of these machinations often look like something seen through a time-space warp: the most ordinary objects take on strange new dimensions.

Toth is also dissatisfied with the results of ordinary color photography. It is not that he objects to things having the color they have; he simply feels limited by the literal-mindedness with which color film records the green of grass or the blue of sky. He wants to be free to choose and manipulate colors in order to emphasize the important elements in his pictures. Consequently he photographs in black and white and afterward imaginatively hand-paints each of his pictures with oil colors.

Now 25 years old, Carl Toth is teaching photography at Cranbrook Academy in Michigan. He studied at the Rochester Institute of Technology and the State University of New York at Buffalo.

From under an elevated highway four different pictures were taken—only two of which included the title subject, the photographer's wife—then joined together to make a single image. The imperfect joints, especially noticeable between the two upper frames, result in disconcerting deformations of space and perspective.

In this picture Toth moved around the girl on the grass and photographed her from four different positions. The feet at the edge of each frame are his. The photographer, the girl and the two dogs at the bottom all seem to inhabit the same space. But the dog at the upper right seems to float upside down in a gravity-free world of its own.

Judy, Ted and Georgie, Bayside, New York, 1972

Here the camera moved from left to right to make a panoramic view of a roadside picnic spot. Each frame has a different perspective, and by combining the three the photographer created a disintegrated world where straight lines curve. The sweet, not-quite-natural color extends through all the frames and serves to unite them.

Judy and Ted on Route 17, New York, 1972

The ridgepole is the only element of the greenhouse roof that is not dislocated by Toth's restless camera, and the far end of the structure is actually shown twice, once at right and once at center left. Yet the pale green of the sky and the shining yellow of the greenhouse rafters provide a color-keyed continuity so that the viewer can easily follow the fractured perspective.

Linda and Ted in a Greenhouse, Buffalo, 1972

This group of pictures, like stills from a movie,
represents a novel expression of space and time.
It is made up of two distinct series of pictures.
In one series, beginning at far left, the camera
sweeps up from green grass to show a dog and
then blue sky beyond. This series alternates with
another in which the motionless camera
records dancing lines on a television screen.

Dog and Television, Buffalo, 1971

The pictures above, like those on the preceding page, resemble motion-picture stills, but are here divided into two groups as though they were facing pages of a book. The two "pages" at the upper left are read first, the two lower left-hand pages next, and then the right-hand upper and lower pictures. Both camera and subject are in motion. The camera starts high in the sky (upper left) and moves down toward the grass. Meanwhile the bicyclist is approaching the photographer and as he does so, he appears to grow larger and larger in each successive frame.

Bicyclist, Buffalo, 1971

In this photograph, a part of the sky, which is colored yellow and green, is separated from the rest of the picture. Below the sky picture, several views of the river are combined: the views on the left look straight across the water, while the scenes at right look down the riverbank.

Judy, Niagara Falls, 1972

When John Banasiak was studying and working in Chicago he used to stop for a beer in this bar on his way home. One night he was struck by the light of the neon signs that seemed to ''scratch away'' the pale blue light of the sky, and he took this picture. This is not the bar he worked and photographed in, but it is the same sort of small neighborhood gathering place he knew so well.

Louie's Bar, Harvey, Illinois, 1972

John Banasiak: Neighborhood Bar

There is a slightly formal yet very friendly feeling about John Banasiak's photographs. The people are clearly posing for him, yet they feel at ease. They are dressed up in their best clothes and they are giving the camera a smile, but they feel no need to make an overpowering impression. They are decent people in a respectable bar where husbands and wives can come together to dance, where fathers may invite young daughters and where nice girls can come alone. Confronted by a camera, and by a photographer who is a friend, they present their best faces to the world, because they have nothing to hide.

All the pictures were taken in the same place, a neighborhood tavern in suburban Chicago that Banasiak had known since he was a child. The bar and the restaurant behind it are a kind of neighborhood social center, he says, "a good place to go to drink, dance, sing and have a good time," and the Polish-descended people of the neighborhood often hold their wedding and funeral receptions and retirement parties there. The photographer grew up in the neighborhood and worked behind the bar while studying photography at the Art Institute of Chicago, and his pictures were taken in the intervals between mixing drinks and talking to customers.

The result, half document, half family snapshot album, is an unusual example of the tendency of many young photographers to use photography as a link between themselves and the rest of the world.

Banasiak's pictures document a world that outsiders know only as a flash of neon lighting and a burst of recorded music as they drive through the anonymous environs of great cities. He has captured this mood of detachment in another series of pictures, like the one on the opposite page, which he took outdoors in color at night. But inside the neighborly tavern, his simple snapshot approach and his warm feeling for people make his own world seem familiar and homey.

Mr. and Mrs. William Dudeck and Sharon, 1972

A Toast, 1972

Behind these two men is the tavern dance floor where they have been dancing with their wives. With fresh drinks, they toast the bartender, who toasts—and photographs—them in return.

Joe and Donna, 1972

The father and daughter in this photograph were attending a silver wedding anniversary party when Banasiak took their picture. The father had recently given up smoking cigars "except on special occasions like when having a beer." Banasiak later poured him a beer and the two of them lit up cigars. The rushing water behind them is part of a beer advertisement.

Last Call, 1972

John Banasiak: Neighborhood Bar

Linda, James and Marcia, 1972

*The man and the girl on the right met in the tavern
at a wedding party, when Banasiak took this
picture; later they began dating and then became
engaged to be married. The life of an entire
neighborhood passed before the young
photographer's camera in the bar, and he
captured it with a tender respect that lends
endless variety to the same simple pictorial idea.*

Carol, Mabel, Barbara, 1972

The four pictures in this group were not all taken at the same time, but together they give the impression of a long view down the bar. Left to right they show: the maid of honor at a wedding party with her parents; a crowd of customers vying for the bartender's attention just before closing time; a pretty girl with a nice smile; the same girl with her sister and grandmother.

Barbara, 1972

The Marketplace

How does the photographer get his pictures out of his darkroom and before the public eye? Unless he is employed by a newspaper or magazine, an advertising agency or an industrial firm that pays him a salary and disseminates his pictures for him, he does it the way any other artist does: by merchandising his wares. Some new ways of merchandising photographs are assuming increasing importance: exhibiting in galleries specializing in the sale of prints; and privately publishing books and portfolios, a venture that more and more photographers are undertaking on their own. In the one instance the photographers have borrowed from painters, who have used galleries as outlets for their works at least since the 19th Century; in the other they have borrowed from poets and novelists, who sometimes hire printers when book publishers turn them away. Both methods involve the techniques of the marketplace. Both require know-how; both are costly; both are gambles. But both offer compensations, financial and otherwise. On the following pages are some of the ventures that made news in the past year.

Inside his storefront Gallery of Photography in North Vancouver, opened in March 1972, Erol Baykal surveys his display of photographs by Art Grice, who owns another gallery across the harbor. Baykal's gallery, like so many spawned by the new interest in photographs as art works, is in an out-of-the-way, low-rent location near the waterfront, and visitors have to hunt for it.

Prints for Sale

In Victorian times, when photographs were novel and seldom engraved for reproduction in books and magazines, an eager public vied to buy handmade, original prints of outstanding scenes, singly or in sets. People stopped buying prints, however, after good reproduction processes came along—until recently, when a renewed interest in photography as an art revived demand for the actual product of the photographic artist. And in 1972 the market for prints was growing fast. Single photographic prints by masters such as Alfred Stieglitz, high priest of photography for nearly half of the 20th Century, fetched as much as $1,000, and works by scores of lesser-known photographers, both living and dead, brought $75 to $750. For the photographer's own handiwork has become a collector's item, exhibited and sold, like other art, in auction rooms—and increasingly, in a recent innovation among marketplaces, the photographic gallery.

Photographic galleries have sprung up everywhere, not only in the art centers of New York, London and Rome, but in scores of other places as well, from Vancouver to São Paulo, from Albuquerque to Tokyo. From only a handful a couple of years ago, their number passed 80 in 1972 and promised to increase further. The men and women who run them play many roles. They act as agents for the established photographer, mentors and financial angels for the fledgling photographer, custodians for the antique photograph, and brokers for the speculator.

What are they like, these new agoras of the photograph? They come in all sizes, from a few hundred square feet with room for a couple of dozen pictures, to several thousand square feet, with room for more than 100; and in a wide range of tastes, from the elegant to the funky. The Light gallery, which opened in New York in November 1971, stands on prestigious Madison Avenue, cheek by jowl with posh salons where paintings sell for more than one million dollars; others are in downtown areas in want of urban renewal. Some galleries lodge in the upstairs quarters of camera shops, where photographers can hardly miss them, but many a gallery sits in an unlikely neighborhood, where casual strollers are neither likely to find them by chance nor apt to be lured by the unlikely neighbors. "I am located across the street from the Mighty Oak Laundromat," says 24-year-old Bennett Scheuer, who opened the Gallery Obsküra in Coconut Grove, Florida, in May 1972, "but how can you put that on an invitation to an exhibit?"

The galleries' activities have as much diversity—and as much in common —as their locations. But they are chiefly in business to display photographs and to sell them. Like the painting galleries on which many of them have modeled themselves, they hold exhibitions, sometimes launched with gala openings embellished by lavish publicity and free-flowing drink designed to promote attendance. "If wine and snacks are served," says Lanfranco Co-

The Pictogramma gallery, which opened in Rome in March 1972, is in the basement of a bookshop. Director Guido Cosulich holds evening workshops at the gallery, where young photographers can take apart and examine new equipment, and learn more about their art by discussing it with older, more experienced photographers.

Three new photo gallery proprietors are seen in their premises: Lee Romero and Donal Holway standing on either side of a partition at the SoHo Photo Gallery, a 120-photographer cooperative in downtown New York; and (bottom) Randolph Laub lolling on a couch in Los Angeles' Ohio Silver gallery, which doubles as his living room.

lombo, who owns Il Diaframma in Milan, "we get about 3,000 people at an opening. Without the trimmings, about 1,000 show up."

When the galleries make sales they usually take commissions for their efforts—from 10 per cent to as much as 40 per cent. A few charge photographers membership dues for the privilege of associating with them, or a hanging fee for exhibiting on their walls. The fee varies widely: it is $100 at The Underground Gallery and $10 at the SoHo Photo Gallery, both in New York. At the Obsküra in Florida, it is $50, but that sum is then subtracted from the commission due the gallery if sales exceed $50.

The boom in the print market notwithstanding, the gallery business remains risky. Three years ago Lee Witkin, a magazine editor and sometime photographer, was able to start the gallery that bears his name in New York on $6,000; in 1972 Erol Baykal needed $10,000 to open in North Vancouver. Witkin, now a sort of elder brother to youthful gallery owners, has grossed a quarter of a million dollars in three years. That is a remarkable sum in a field where during the same period more than half a dozen new galleries went under in the United States alone. In Milwaukee photographer Roald Bostrom opened the Bathhouse Gallery in late 1969; in 1972 he said mournfully that his enterprise "was successful in every way but financial." He lured some of the same big-name photographers that Witkin deals with in New York, and said he "had to keep trimming the mailing list for openings" because the crowds were too big to handle; but he lost upwards of $20,000 in two and a half years, and in June closed down. Financial aid may be an answer, but not necessarily. Germany's Album-Fotogalerie, in a picturesque and quiet house beyond a plant-filled courtyard in Ehrenfeld, a small neighborhood of Cologne, has been offered municipal aid; but the owners stubbornly turn it down because they insist on remaining independent in their choice of photographs, and they fear the strings that generally come attached to financial aid from government—or other—sources.

Most gallery owners consider themselves lucky to sell half a dozen prints from a single exhibit, which usually runs three weeks or a month. "Visitors tend to treat the gallery as a little museum," says Guido Cosulich, who directs the Pictogramma in Rome. "They walk around and enjoy the photos as a cultural treat, but the idea of buying one doesn't seem to occur to them. Perhaps we would get a better response if I labeled the pictures 'Not for Sale.' " These problems force galleries to look elsewhere for supplementary income. Some provide educational services, others sell photographic books and portfolios, and a few offer photographic equipment; most of these galleries welcome browsers. "Not too many people can afford the Paul Strand monograph at $40," says Bennett Scheuer, who sells books to supplement print sales at the Obsküra, "but at least there is a place they can see

The F/Stop gallery, which opened in Palo Alto, California, in July, has one distinction not commonly found in galleries: It rents a darkroom to beginning photographers. The income from that service, combined with fees for classes in photography, helps support the gallery.

Owner Bennett Scheuer sits cross-legged on the ▶ floor of his Gallery Obskúra in Coconut Grove, Florida (right), among some of the pictures he has on sale. Because galleries are rarely lucrative, he drives a bakery truck to make ends meet and hires someone else to mind the gallery.

WALKER EVANS
JULY 26 - AUG 20

At the Mind's Eye gallery in Vancouver, co-owner Art Grice contemplates an exhibit of Walker Evans photographs of the 1930s. The gallery is located in Gastown, Vancouver's oldest neighborhood —currently undergoing a facelifting, and thereby acquiring boutiques, tourists and glamor as an addition to some remaining derelicts.

On its skylighted upper deck, The Floating ▶ Foundation of Photography, a houseboat that plies the Hudson River in New York, exhibits the work of unusually disparate photographers. At different times may be seen pictures made by prison inmates and mental patients as well as by widely known professional photographers.

it in south Florida now. Besides, *I* can't afford half the books in my gallery."

One offbeat gallery does live on grants; that is The Floating Foundation of Photography, which gets both state and private philanthropic aid for teaching photography—as therapy for inmates of Sing Sing prison, patients of a mental hospital and high-school dropouts. The gallery does float; it is a purple, yellow and white houseboat based in a marina in the Hudson River off Manhattan. Getting a berth there was a feat; the proprietor feared that the garish paint job would distract motorists on the expressway nearby and cause accidents. Not until the resourceful director, Maggie Sherwood, enlisted the sympathy of the New York City Parks Commissioner was the matter settled. When the boat ties up at its regular sites along the river (other than Sing Sing), any interested viewer can go aboard—and some 85,000 have done so in the two years that the boat has been in operation. From time to time they can see exhibits of well-known photographers as well as works by the foundation's pupils. As at other galleries, photographs are for sale but, instead of a commission for showing or selling them, Mrs. Sherwood asks, from those who can afford it, for a contribution to the boat. She once received a bottle of wine in lieu of a cash offering.

More conventional are the educational efforts of other galleries, which generally provide lectures and seminars where beginners can find expert advice and compare their work with that of their peers. Because darkroom equipment is fragile and expensive, few galleries provide it; they expect the photographers to fit themselves out on their own. But the Baldwin Street Gallery in Toronto is an exception to that rule. The gallery is an eight-woman cooperative run by photographer Laura Jones, who keeps her own darkroom open 24 hours a day—for the use of women only. She believes that many women take up photography because their husbands or men friends engage in it, only to find themselves excluded from its practice by prejudice.

But selling photographs, not instructing photographers, has been the source of the success of the most prosperous American gallery, Lee Witkin's. Careful business management is an essential ingredient, however. The biggest mistake that prospective gallery owners make, Witkin believes, is overspending on rent for a fancy address (his own gallery, though hardly in poverty quarters, is several blocks off New York's main art-gallery circuit).

Witkin has also been able to acquire a rich clientele. His patrons are not only art lovers in search of decoration for their own homes, but also museum curators seeking historic photographs for posterity, and investors with plenty of money to spend in the bullish photographic market. And plenty of money is being spent, not only in the galleries, but in other kinds of places where photographs are sold these days.

The prestigious art auction house of Sotheby's in London, for instance, has for some years been including photographs and photographic equipment among its general auctions of antiques. In December 1971 it held the first sale devoted exclusively to photography, and in August 1972 it held a second. "It took a year to accumulate the material for that first auction," says Phillipe Garner, the young Englishman who heads Sotheby's photographic department; few owners of photographs bothered to bring in prints for sale at the first auction. "It took only six months for the latest one." At the latter auction, sales totaled $35,000, a formidable sum for a collection of photographic items. Of that sum, $12,000 alone went for a single album of 32 prints made by the Scottish team of David Octavius Hill and Robert Adamson between 1843 and 1848, using the then popular but now half-forgotten paper-negative process called calotype.

At another recent sale the print on the opposite page, by the 19th Century British photographer Julia Margaret Cameron, brought nearly $700, and that sale illustrates even better what is happening to photographic prices. Only a few years ago a Metropolitan Museum of Art curator returned from England with 150 photographs by the same lady; he had paid $150 for the lot.

On the gallery circuit, where prints by living photographers are for sale, inflation is similarly setting in. Three years ago a signed print by Edward Steichen fetched the then high sum of $500; today it would bring $1,000, and so would good prints by Paul Strand *(pages 11-33)* and his contemporary László Moholy-Nagy. A photograph by Aaron Siskind, who has taught hundreds of today's major photographers, could be had for as little as $50 two years ago; today his prints bring as much as $250. If prices keep going up at present rates—and the signs are that they will—the far-sighted among today's gallerygoers stand to make some healthy investments for the future.

With the ease of a man who has made it, Lee Witkin reclines in a desk chair at his New York gallery in front of an array of high-priced photographs. The Witkin Gallery is the most successful of the new galleries specializing in photographs, and his main problem today is explaining to tyros why he cannot handle their work: his bins are overflowing, and he has shows scheduled two years in advance of their opening.

At Christie's art auction house in London, where ▶ zooming prices for photographic prints have documented the boom that gave birth to photo galleries around the world, a 19th Century photograph goes under the gavel for nearly $700. The picture, of Sir John Herschel, the scientist-of-many-parts who coined the word photography, was made by his versatile contemporary, the portraitist and illustrator Julia Margaret Cameron.

Self-Publishing

In 1972 more and more photographers were finding new and inventive ways of putting their pictures before the public. Many were venturing into independent publishing, or "self-publishing," that is, printing and distributing their photographs in books and portfolios, in postcard or wall-poster sizes, with or without accompanying text. Books and portfolios of photographs have of course been produced before by commercial publishing houses; the difference is that now photographers are undertaking to do the publishing themselves. They began in the latter 1960s, when they found that many cost-conscious publishers were reluctant to gamble on the work of new and untried photographers. In taking on their own publishing, the photographers are themselves becoming entrepreneurs as well as artists, dealing with dollars and cents, profit and loss—all the risks of businessmen.

When the photographer takes up publishing on his own, he confronts a formidable array of problems. He has to raise the money, engage a printer, decide on a format, choose the paper, stand over the press to be sure the result is as he wants it, devise ways of promoting the product and methods of distributing it. For the latter he may engage a house that specializes in mail-order distribution; such firms already have an entree to the market and the know-how for exploiting it, and the photographer pays a varying commission for their services. Or he may leave his newly minted work on consignment with a gallery, a museum or a bookstore, which will usually charge him nothing for shelf space but take a cut of 40 per cent or more on sales. The photographer can send copies of his book or portfolio to critics who write for newspapers and magazines, hoping for a favorable review; but even if he does get one it is no guarantee of sales. One photographer had the disheartening experience of being favorably reviewed, only to discover that readers were given no idea of where to buy his book (he had not arranged to sell it through the bookstores).

Few photographers make money on their independent publishing. Photographer George Krause estimates that it cost him $12,000 to publish his book *(page 160)* and to date he has sold only 300 copies at $9.75 apiece. Of the production cost, $10,500 went for printing alone, and he considers that a bargain; a different printer had bid for the job at twice the amount. Besides the printing, there are added costs for mailing and publicity and a stipend for someone to write introductory or other text.

But the compensations must outweigh the costs and the risks, because more and more photographers are undertaking the publication of their own work. The photographer who does so has the tangible satisfaction of seeing his pictures in print, and of knowing that he created both the contents and their presentation. Finally, in self-publishing, as in horse racing, there is always the seductive hope that the gamble will pay off in financial terms.

Privately published works by four different ▶ photographers indicate recent trends in marketing. From top left, they are a book with photographs and text, a book of photographs only and a portfolio of postcard-sized pictures; at right is a collection of poster-sized pictures. More about them appears on the following pages.

Duncan's Portfolio

David Douglas Duncan, who has published books on his own, in 1972 chose one of the oldest ways of presenting photographs: in a portfolio of separate pictures. But he brought the portfolio up to date by reproducing the pictures in color and size—17¼ by 24½ inches —large enough to hang on the wall yet, because they are reproductions rather than actual prints, reasonable in price.

Out of the thousands of photographs Duncan has taken during the course of 35 years—picturing everything from the sordidness of war to the beauty of peaceful landscapes—he chose 12 that he hoped would have a universal appeal. They focus mainly on human beings—a potter in Morocco, a young couple boating on a Paris lagoon, women praying in a Cairo mosque—but there is also a picture of sheep in Ireland and one of Notre Dame in Paris. All exhibit a serene beauty remote from worldly suffering. He calls his work simply *Portfolio*. It is priced at $25 and is sold by Neiman-Marcus, Dallas, Texas, and Halls, Kansas City, Missouri.

Tribesman, Hindu Kush mountains, Afghanistan, 1955

Tadjiks on Review, Moscow, 1958

◄ In an unearthly setting of striated mountains and rippled reflections, an Afghan tribesman tends to the mundane business of washing dishes in a central Afghanistan river. The scene appears timeless, but is merely a suspended moment: The tribesman must move on, the reflections shift and only the remote mountains will stay unchanged.

In a picture reminiscent of an ancient frieze, Turkoman horsemen from Central Asia parade across a carpet of brightly dyed sand in the hippodrome in Moscow. The ceremony, where intent seems to have been to surpass the pageantry of former tsars, opened the celebration of May Day, the main Soviet labor holiday.

155

Krims: A Box of Deerslayers

Leslie Krims put his pictures in boxes, arranged in groups according to specific themes, or to tell a story.

The ones shown here are from a set of 24 he calls *The Deerslayers,* in a paraphrase of the classic frontier novel by James Fenimore Cooper. But Leslie Krims's deerslayers are modern hunters shown with their prey. He stationed himself on a well-traveled New York state highway during the deer-hunting seasons of 1970 and 1971 and photographed hunters en route home from the chase, each with his trophy securely lashed to his car.

The Deerslayers was put on sale in 1972 in two versions. One is a collection of 5-by-5⅝-inch reproductions priced at $3.50; the other is a much more elaborate affair costing $1,000 and containing samples of deerhide with original photographic prints that are 14 by 17 inches in size, signed, numbered and mounted on mat board. Both may be obtained by mail order from Light Impressions, P.O. Box 3012, Rochester, New York 14614.

From *The Deerslayers*, 1972

Winningham: "Going Texan"

Geoff Winningham thinks books are just the place for photographs—partly because he believes a supplementary text to be an asset to the images, partly because he believes that the pictures in a book, when carefully produced, can match the beauty of photographs printed singly and by hand. So he raised the money to publish one himself: *Going Texan,* a photographic study of an annual celebration called "Going Texan Days," which takes place in Houston toward the end of February.

The event, Winningham says, is a "Texan Mardi Gras," with a parade, square dances and the disorder of carnivals; but its major attractions are a rodeo and a show of livestock raised by Texas teenagers, who compete for prizes and for auction sales. Winningham set out to record the physical magnificence of the animals and the pioneer energy of rural Texas youths in photographs and the words of the participants. The book, with text written by Rice University sociologist William C. Martin from Winningham's interviews, sells for $20. It can be had by writing direct to Geoff Winningham, P.O. Box 25271, Houston, Texas 77005.

Young Texans sit still while local artists commemorate their presence at the Houston rodeo and livestock show. A finished pastel portrait cost each budding cattleman three dollars.

To get this prizewinning pig where the photographer wanted it, under the banner naming the show, a bowl of food was pulled along the platform. He hoped that the pig would look up but the food proved too attention-getting, and Winningham shot this portrait of a champion absorbed in its meal.

'An Appaloosa horse named Jokers Wild stands together with its trainer and "Miss National Appaloosa Queen 1972" in a barn at the Texas fair. The Queen's pants suit echoes Jokers Wild's piebald coat, and is also a visual pun on the name of the breed: it is printed with apples.

Krause's Favorites

Birds, Mexico, 1964

When Krause saw these birds perched in the window of a bird shop in Mexico, he was not so much interested by them as by a light bulb at the top of the cage. But having made the photograph, he disliked it, and he set it aside. Eight years later he suddenly realized that cropping the photograph to remove the light bulb would make an entirely different picture. So he cropped—and got this scene suggesting birds in reverie.

To reach a wide audience and allow them to share a glimpse of his very personal and rather fantastical vision of the world, commercial photographer George Krause put up his own money for the publication of a collection of his black-and-white photographs in a book that he titled simply *George Krause-1*.

What predominates in Krause's photographic vision is the narrow margin that falls between reality and fantasy, and he tries to capture moments when actual and familiar elements suddenly begin to be transformed into unworldly images that are still, however, real. "After all," he says, "I could not photograph what wasn't there."

George Krause's book sells for $9.75 and it is available by mail request from the photographer himself, who lives at 137 South Eighth Street, Philadelphia, Pennsylvania 19106.

Church Window, Moosehead Lake, Maine, 1963

The window of a New England church frames a
little girl who unconcernedly gazes at a leafy bush
outside, while an older woman, haloed in light
behind her, seems lost in contemplation.

The Door, Seville, Spain, 1963

A knocker in the shape of a hand and a girl
standing in the shadow of a doorway studded with
six doorknobs seem to be guarding the entrance
to a dark and spectral world beyond.

161

The photographer spied these sheep being turned out to graze after a night's shelter in a mountain cave. He climbed up to get the perspective he wanted and then, just as the last two sheep appeared, he captured the scene in a modern photograph that could have been an illustration of Cyclops' sheep emerging from their cave.

GEORGE KRAUSE: *The Cave of Sheep*, Estremoz, Portugal, 1970

The Annual Awards

Art and Courage 166

Practically everywhere in the world where there are cameras, awards are given annually for the year's best work in photography. From Aalborg to Zagreb, amateur camera clubs and professional associations single out the work of one or two of their members for special recognition. The subject matter of the prize-winning pictures ranges widely, from the most appealing picture of a baby taking its first steps to the most revealing picture taken with a scanning electron microscope.

Few award-winning photographers—or examples of their work—ever attract national or international attention. The handful that do are usually professionals, either photographers for the press or established freelance masters of the camera. The prestigious prizes they strive for are, in the United States, the Robert Capa Award, the National Press Photographers Association "Photographer of the Year," the American Society of Magazine Photographers and the Pulitzer citations; in France, the Niepce prize; in Japan, the Nihon Shashin Kyokai awards; and in Germany, the Kulturpreis and the David Octavius Hill medal. The work of the photographers who received these distinguished honors in 1972 is shown on the following pages.

Robert Capa Award—U.S.A. ►
"For superlative still photography requiring exceptional courage and enterprise," the Robert Capa Award was given posthumously to Larry Burrows in 1972, for nearly a decade's coverage of the war in Southeast Asia. His courage and enterprise cost him his life. One of his most poignant and memorable picture narratives concluded with this photograph of a grieving airman whose comrades had died in a mission on a helicopter named "Yankee Papa 13." On February 10, 1971, Burrows and three colleagues were reported missing and presumed dead after their helicopter was shot down over Laos.

LARRY BURROWS: *After a Mission*, 1965

Art and Courage

Because newspapers since the latter part of the 19th Century have made the widest practical and commercial use of photographs in print, press pictures take many of the awards given every year for excellence in photography. But because good news photographs must be arresting, provocative and story-telling, they almost always depict violence and tragedy; as a result, press photography awards are usually commendations for conspicuous bravery —because the photographers had the courage to be *there*—as well as for photojournalistic acumen. The prize winners of 1972 were no exceptions —war dominated news photography just as it dominated the news.

Many other prizes, however, are given for esthetic merit. These include Germany's David Octavius Hill medal and France's two Niepce awards. They were named for two innovators in the field (Hill, a Scot, was a pioneer famous for his calotype portraits and Joseph-Nicéphore Niepce is credited with the invention of the medium in 1822). Artistic creativity with the camera is also the criterion for Japan's three Nihon Shashin Kyokai awards, named for the organization that presents them—the Japan Photography Society. Any type of subject matter and any style of photography is eligible. In 1972, such esthetic awards went for pictures that included, as might be expected, symbolic abstracts *(pages 172, 174 and 175)*—but also a brilliant, glossy fashion photograph *(page 176)*.

While some awards are given for a single outstanding picture, most are given to a photographer for achieving a consistently high level in a large body of work. In 1972, LIFE photographer Larry Burrows won the Robert Capa medal from the Overseas Press Club for almost ten years of relentlessly difficult and hazardous coverage of the war in Indochina. Twice before, Burrows had won the Capa award—in 1966 and 1969; this time the prize was given posthumously, only months after Burrows disappeared in a helicopter crash over Laos. Ironically, he died only a few hundred miles from the spot where the man in whose memory the award is given, famous photojournalist Robert Capa, was killed 17 years earlier covering the fighting between the Vietnamese Communists and the French.

Pictures of a different war won another of the most important prizes in 1972—for two photographers instead of one. Horst Faas and Michel Laurent, both covering the aftermath of the fighting in Bangladesh for the Associated Press, were photographing a victory rally that turned into a savage spectacle. As Pakistani captives were kicked, beaten and stabbed to death, Faas and Laurent shot pictures at a furious rate. Afterward they tried to sort out their exposed film and put it in order. "Have you shot any color?" Faas asked his colleague. "I don't know," Laurent answered. In the turmoil, neither had been able to keep track of his film. In the end, they pooled their pictures —and shared a Pulitzer Prize *(page 171)*.

ROBERT W. MADDEN: *June Week at Annapolis*, 1971

Photographer of the Year—U.S.A.

The year's only press photography prizewinner to consist of cheerful pictures was a story on Maryland by Robert W. Madden; he was named Photographer of the Year by the University of Missouri and the National Press Photographers Association. This picture shows a rite in which Naval Academy plebes climb a greased monument.

ERNST HAAS: *Summer*, 1964

American Society of Magazine Photographers Award—U.S.A.

The ASMP saluted Ernst Haas as "one of the most influential photographers of his generation." Germany's Photographic Society also gave him its Kulturpreis. This dreamlike depiction of a meadow appeared in his book The Creation.

WOLFGANG PETER GELLER: *Death of Bank Robber Vicenik,* 1971

**Press Photo of the Year Award
—The Netherlands**

*"For bravery and perseverance in the line of
duty,"* the World Press Photo jury cited 26-year-
old German freelance Wolfgang Peter Geller for
the picture above. The last of a series, it shows a
gangster dying, hit by a policeman's bullet.

DAVE KENNERLY: *Soldier in Vietnam,* 1971

**Pulitzer Prize for
Feature Photography—U.S.A.**

*One of the two Pulitzer prizes in photography
awarded in 1972 went to 25-year-old Dave
Kennerly for his general coverage of the war in
Indochina. This example, taken in Vietnam during
a deceptively quiet moment, shows a GI poised
with his rifle at the edge of a defoliated forest.*

HORST FAAS and MICHEL LAURENT: *Death in Dacca, 1972*

Pulitzer Prize for Spot News—U.S.A.

Because they worked so closely and could not distinguish which film was whose, German-born Horst Faas and Frenchman Michel Laurent shared a Pulitzer Prize. Their pictures of the postwar Bangladesh vengeance, in which a Pakistani captive was bayoneted to death in front of a crowd, revealed the savagery of that bitter war.

171

GUILLAUME LIEURY: *The Infernal Machine*—from ''The Penal Colony''—1971

Le Prix Niepce—France

*France's foremost photographic prize—usually
given to one photographer and always to
someone young and upcoming—was presented in
1972 to two youthful photographers. Guillaume
Lieury, just 21 in 1972, won one of the awards for
enigmatic scenes like this shadowy figure
dwarfed by the machinery of a ski lift. Because
of its nightmarish mood, he named it for
part of a work by surrealist writer Franz Kafka.*

PIERRE LE GALL: *La Salle d'Attente*, 1971

Le Prix Niepce—France

A second Prix Niepce was awarded to 24-year-old Pierre Le Gall, a teacher of philosophy in the city of Dieppe. Le Gall's pictures all have philosophical overtones: this juxtaposition of a man seated in a railroad station waiting room in Le Havre warily watching the ghostly figure of a window washer, Le Gall feels, expresses the solitude of individuals and their difficulties in communicating with one another.

HISAHARU TAGA: *Wild Barley on the Tottori Dunes*, 1968

KON SASAKI: *Birth of Octopus Vulgaris*, 1967

Nendo Sho (Annual Award)—Japan

One of four awards given by Japan's Shashin Kyokai (Photography Society) went to 53-year-old Hisaharu Taga for "results of more than 10 years' efforts to capture the spirit of the sand dunes" of Tottori. As this example reveals, he depicted the dunes in a succinct, typically Japanese manner.

Nendo Sho (Annual Award)—Japan

Beautiful and informative photomicrographs of minute forms of life won a Shashin Kyokai prize for veteran science photographer Kon Sasaki. A collection of 75 of Sasaki's remarkable pictures, including the one above showing octopuses at birth, was made into a book entitled Tiny Life.

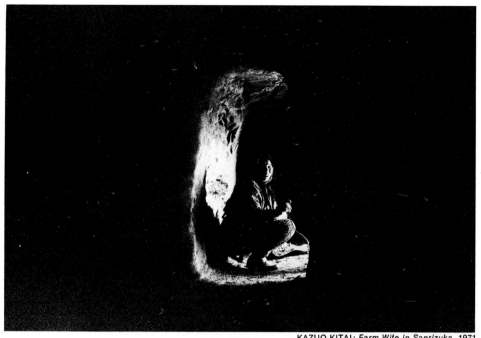

KAZUO KITAI: *Farm Wife in Sanrizuka*, 1971

Shinjin Sho (Newcomer Award)—Japan

For "spotlighting a serious social issue," the one prize Shashin Kyokai gives to an upcoming photographer went to 26-year-old Kazuo Kitai for coverage of the militant families of Sanrizuka who refused to vacate their farms for an airport. At left, a woman guards supplies stored in a cave.

Nendo Sho (Annual Award)—Japan

"For recording the scenery of the Chichibu mountains and the people there," an award went to Buko Shimizu, a onetime news photographer who gave up city life to make a study of his native province. This example shows a cluster of snow-capped stone Buddhas in a temple compound.

BUKO SHIMIZU: *A Snowy Day*, 1968

REGINA RELANG: *Model with a Reflector*, 1971

David Octavius Hill Award—Germany

Germany's most prestigious prize—given for outstanding artistic merit in any field of photography—was awarded to Regina Relang for the excellence of all her work. The striking threefold portrait of a fashion model's face repeated in a polished metal sun reflector represents the originality and high standards of Mrs. Relang's fashion photographs.

The Year's Books

In the past year some 30 new photographic books came onto the market —more than have ever before been introduced in a single year. Almost every one of the new books contains the work of a single photographer and, reflecting the current preference of most photographers, all but a few of the books carry only black-and-white pictures. Their sizes, formats and prices vary greatly, however; there are several small, paperbound books containing 10 or 20 pictures and selling for less than five dollars, as well as a number of large volumes that include more than 100 reproductions and are priced as high as $40.

On the following pages four of the outstanding books of 1972 are represented. The photographers whose work they encompass—André Kertész, Margaret Bourke-White, George Tice and Elliott Erwitt—are briefly discussed and selections from each book are reproduced. For a listing of the other important photography books of 1972, see page 214.

An experimenter throughout his career, André Kertész took the picture at right with one hand extended to hold the camera and the other resting affectionately on the shoulder of his wife-to-be. The resulting portrait is the frontispiece for a 1972 retrospective book on Kertész's work.

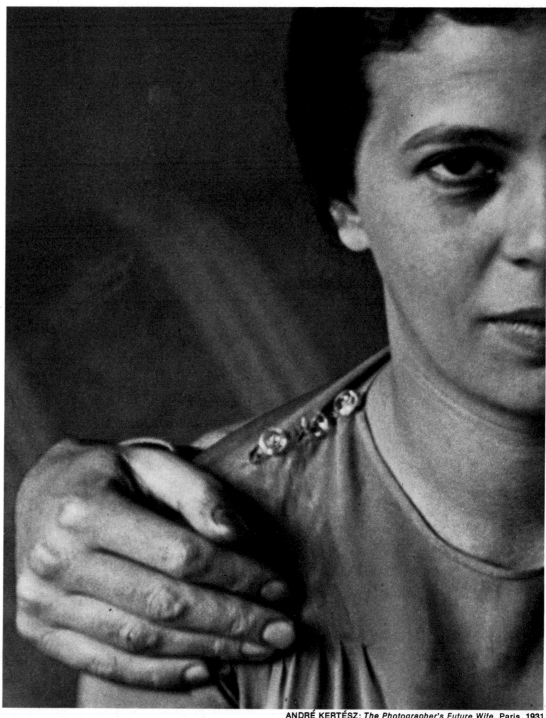

ANDRÉ KERTÉSZ: *The Photographer's Future Wife*, Paris, 1931

"André Kertész: 1912-1972"

A pioneer of candid photography and one of the first great photojournalists, André Kertész is best known as a wry poet of common humanity, the creator of a panorama of ordinary life seen from a slightly offbeat point of view. There are, however, other aspects of the photographer that are not so well known, and one of the merits of the new album of his work, *André Kertész: 1912-1972,* is that it shows them all.

The book contains many pictures that are thought of as distinctively Kertész—scenes of New York, for instance, in which the anonymity and coldness of a great modern city gives way to such a delightful small-scale happening as a human arm emerging from an exhaust fan. Along with this kind of Kertész, however, there are many other different kinds—so many others that the viewer begins to wonder which André Kertész is the real one.

The first Kertész was not a poet of humanity at all. In 1912, when he started out, photojournalism was still an art of the future, and any photographer who wanted to be taken seriously photographed stately landscapes or figure compositions for exhibition in the salons. The first thing Kertész did was to make himself a master of the salon style. A native of Budapest, he wandered around his picturesque city and the Hungarian countryside looking for likely locations, and the early pictures in this book include hushed views of hazy parks, melting snows and reflections and ripples in lily ponds.

People only began to figure prominently in his work during the First World War, which put him into the Austro-Hungarian army and sent him over much of Eastern Europe, and his first pictures of soldiers opened his eyes to the importance of daily life. Thereafter, his landscapes were imbued with the presence of people, and he began to create the record of everyday life in Hungary that is one of the most beautiful and moving sections of the book.

Then in 1925 he went to Paris. It was thrilling to be an artist in Paris in the '20s. The modern movement was in full swing, and Kertész experimented along with the rest. He continued to photograph the street and village life that had fascinated him in Hungary, but he also documented the lives of the artists. His portraits, and views of the studios of such celebrities as the Dutch painter Piet Mondrian, are an invaluable record of a heroic period.

It was in Paris that Kertész became a professional; up to then he had worked as a clerk in the Budapest Bourse and photographed as a hobby. Photojournalism was just getting started in Europe in the '30s, and improvisation was the rule; photographers were planning and shooting their own stories with little advice from editors. Such assignments suited Kertész. He was famous even then for taking the unexpected approach, and soon he was freelancing for all the leading European newspapers and for the new picture magazines that were just beginning publication. By the time he was 40 he was the idol of most of the younger photographers, and was acknowledged

ANDRÉ KERTÉSZ: 1912-1972
Photographs by André Kertész. Introduction by Paul Dermée. Edited by Nicolas Ducrot. 205 pages. Grossman Publishers, New York, 1972. $19.95

as master by such rising newcomers as Brassaï and Cartier-Bresson.

Then in 1936 Kertész came to New York with a two-year contract to work for a picture agency. He had not intended to stay in New York for more than two years; but the outbreak of World War II cut him off from Europe, and he took a job making fashion photographs and pictures of fashionable interiors, pictures he did not consider representative of his best art—they are not included in the retrospective book. By the 1940s, magazine photography had become a well-organized and highly specialized profession that no longer afforded its old freedom for roving dispositions such as his. He worked hard and long, and eventually made a material success. But his first years in New York were not happy. It took him a long time to find his way back to the puckish insouciance of his early photographs and, by the time he did, an odd thing had happened: the New York of his pictures had taken on the leisurely lineaments of the half-remembered Europe of his early years.

So which Kertész is the real one? The 224 photographs selected by editor Nicolas Ducrot for the book make the most comprehensive collection of his pictures ever published, the first to do justice to his work as a whole. And they suggest that the real Kertész is a whole that is greater than the sum of all his parts. He is an artist with an unerring sense of form, but he is also a blithe and antic spirit. His feeling for living creatures is deep and warm, but he approaches the world with an eye for the unexpected and the incongruous. He is a loving interpreter of the world of his youth and of his early maturity, but he has brought to America, his third and last home, the same genial spirit and impeccable sense of design that make all his pictures a delight to the eye and a joy to the heart.

As an infantryman in the Hungarian army during World War I, the young Kertész (below, second from right) made friends with villagers—including these smiling Albanians—everywhere his platoon was stationed. At 78 (below, right), he talks animatedly in the study of his New York apartment, surrounded by mementos and art objects accumulated during his colorful career.

Intrigued by the goings-on behind a high board
fence, a young Hungarian couple share a knothole
to gain a free view of a circus. They were so
absorbed by what they saw that they took no
notice of the photographer close behind them.
With the small camera he carried wherever he
went, he caught their rapt, childlike attentiveness.

The photograph at right, of Kertész' brother ▶
Eugene in a pond outside Budapest, is an
intentional visual puzzle: Which way is up? And
which is real, the head or the reflection? The
picture as printed is the upside-down image that
Kertész saw in the ground-glass screen of his
view camera; he simply chose to publish it
reversed, with the reflection dominating the
composition and the swimmer's head seeming to
be hardly more than a curious adjunct to it.

Circus, Budapest, 1920

Reflection, Duna Haraszti, 1919

Iskola Ter, Budapest, 1920

The tranquillity of this little park in Budapest is
conveyed by the stillness of the seated figure, the
near-symmetry of the bare-branched trees,
and the serene, foursquare lines of the empty
schoolhouse. Although this was not the
photographer's own neighborhood, it was one of
his favorite places for wandering because
its simple buildings and the hilly terrain made his
native city seem like a peaceful village.

Exploring his adopted home of Paris, just as he ▶
had earlier explored Budapest, Kertész recorded
its obscure outskirts as well as its well-known
sites. In suburban Meudon (right), a high-flown
viaduct caught his eye—and the whistle of
an approaching train signaled him to wait for the
moment when a steam engine chugged into
the center of the scene, adding another flurry of
activity to the bustle of the streets below.

Meudon, France, 1928

Chez Mondrian, Paris, 1926

186

In this interior view of the home of Dutch painter Piet Mondrian (left) the photographer summed up the paradoxical qualities of warmth and aloofness that were two sides of Mondrian's personality. At the same time, Kertész was guided by Mondrian's art, in which forms and tones are arranged in precise balance and proportion.

The faces of two ancient marble busts assume an appearance of intense concentration as they stare out of a third-story window in Paris. The photographer spied them from the street below and was amused by their serious demeanor; in fact they were just a wigmaker's dummies.

Window, Paris, 1928

While on a magazine assignment to photograph art collector Peggy Guggenheim, Kertész took this picture for himself. It depicts the slightly dizzy world of the eccentric heiress by showing her in the curving surface of a concave mirror, surrounded by her possessions and at the same time possessed by them; her image is almost dwarfed by the giant shadow of an ornate vase.

Peggy Guggenheim, New York City, 1945

A lion made of painted wood leers with false ferocity through the window of an antique shop in New York. Kertész was charmed by the beast's comical expression and the tilt of its head. When he looked at the scene in his viewfinder, however, he thought it seemed to lack something. So in order to balance the composition he incorporated another figure into the scene: his own shadow.

Dangerous Animal, Southport, New York, 1949

Sheep, Paris, 1931

*Always attracted to animals, the photographer
was touched by the helpless resignation implicit
in this forlorn trio waiting to be sold at auction;
somehow, they look all the more pitiful for having
been recently sheared. His pictures of animals,
whatever seems to be their mood, consistently
reveal Kertész' affection for all living creatures.*

Seemingly severed from its owner's body, the arm of a repairman protrudes through the blades of a drugstore's exhaust fan. Although Kertész himself refuses to interpret its symbolism, the viewer can hardly miss the message in this strange juxtaposition: a melancholy comment on the depersonalizing effect of machines on men.

Fan, New York, 1937

This photograph, like those on pages 193 and 196, demonstrates Kertész' uncanny talent for spotting pictures while gazing out of windows. Here the window framed the jarring contrast between the giddy smile of a billboard model and the self-contained solemnity of the faceless passersby on the opposite side of the street.

"Buy," New York, 1962

Winding through an intersection like an Oriental dragon with an arrow for a tail, a group of umbrella-bearing Japanese go their separate ways in a rainstorm. Like so many of Kertész' pictures, this one was the result of coincidence. On the day he received a new lens it rained, and he was confined to his hotel room. Looking out the window through the viewfinder, he spotted this parade of pedestrians and snapped the shutter at the precise moment when the picture's elements fell into a pattern of serpentine grace.

Rainy Day, Tokyo, 1968

Although Kertész does not usually arrange pictures, for this one he placed a weather-beaten fence post, retrieved from a trash heap, in front of a copy of a Rubens portrait. Seen through the gnarled opening left for a fence rail, the portrait's staid subject looks like a capricious wood sprite.

Untitled, 1959

While studying the patterns left by demolition of a building in Manhattan, the photographer noticed a pigeon hovering over the site. After three tries he managed to catch the bird in mid-flight, silhouetting it against the scarred wall like a pressed flower between the pages of a book.

Landing Pigeon, New York, 1960

Winter Garden, New York, 1970

The harmonious geometry of snow fencing
and bare tree branches in New York's Washington
Square Park is the product of one of the
photographer's few experiments in darkroom
manipulation. The original negative included only
the left half of this picture, but in printing he
joined the original version to its mirror image.

Breakfasting on the balcony of a Caribbean hotel, the ▶
78-year-old photographer was intrigued by
the shadowy forms of people moving about on the
next balcony behind a translucent glass divider. At one
point a hotel guest paused to lean on the railing,
providing in his rounded, almost abstract form
a counterbalance for a massive rectangle of sky.

On Martinique, 1972

"The Photographs of Margaret Bourke-White"

Margaret Bourke-White was a natural subject for legends while she was alive, and *The Photographs of Margaret Bourke-White* helps explain why most of the stories about her were true. One legend made her a glamorous, ambitious woman (she was almost as good a subject as she was a photographer) who went to any lengths, and put herself in all kinds of physical peril, to get the pictures she wanted. First as a contributor to FORTUNE and later as one of the first staff photographers on LIFE, she competed—successfully —in what was regarded as a man's domain, the world of photojournalism. She cajoled officials to let her ride on bombing missions during World War II —the first woman to do so. She dropped down mine shafts in South Africa, and when she recovered from the dead faint caused by oppressive airlessness, got her pictures. She forced herself to walk through German concentration camps as gamely as she wriggled on the Kremlin floor to coax a twinkle of life onto Josef Stalin's stony face.

Bourke-White was determined and courageous; nothing stopped her, not even the 19-year battle against Parkinson's disease that ended only with her death in 1971. But more than determination is needed for great pictures. As the 200 or so pictures in the new book show, Bourke-White possessed a masterful sense of composition, notable from almost the beginning of her career —particularly in the early photographs of industry *(opposite and following pages)* that made mundane factories and workshops into dramatic pieces of art. One critic remarked that she could transform an American factory into a Gothic cathedral. She filled a frame as a painter covers a canvas with a broad brush, using bold, prime colors. No matter what her subject, she approached it with an eye alert to its surface patterns and its inner rhythms. It was this sense of design that gives her pictures the forcefulness that unmistakably identifies each one as a Bourke-White.

THE PHOTOGRAPHS OF
MARGARET BOURKE-WHITE
Foreword by Carl Mydans. Introduction by
Theodore M. Brown. Edited by Sean Callahan. 208
pages. New York Graphic Society, Greenwich,
Connecticut, 1972. $15.

Dwarfed by the spokes of a gigantic steel ▶
spider web, the worker at lower left examines the
rivets of a section of culvert being built to
divert water from the Missouri River for a flood-
control and irrigation project. The picture came
from the "take" the photographer made for LIFE's
first cover story, on the construction of the
mammoth dam in Fort Peck, Montana.

Garment District, New York, 1930

For an early FORTUNE story called "Cloak and Suit," Bourke-White photographed clothing workers milling in the streets of New York's garment district during their lunch break. She shot straight down from a high floor in a skyscraper, transforming the hatted clothiers into what looks like bees buzzing busily around their hive.

In the early days of the Roosevelt administration, the photographer was assigned by the Newspaper Enterprise Association, a picture and feature service, to do a story on Washington, D.C. The grandeur of the staircase of the Capitol fascinated her, and in this photograph she depicted it not as a grand, upward sweep, but as a series of stark stripes curving outward toward infinity.

Capitol Steps, Washington, 1935

The original caption for this photograph, which occupied a full page in an early issue of FORTUNE, explained simply: "Here are 86,048 spindles with a spinning capacity of 150,000 pounds of yarn a week." Bourke-White depicted this sea of machinery as a single vast expanse of fabric with the figures of wool-factory workers woven directly into its warp and woof.

American Woolen Co., New England, 1935

George A. Tice: "Paterson"

Paterson, New Jersey, an unlovely city, was the subject of one of the hand-somest photographic books of 1972: *Paterson,* by George A. Tice. Its 66 black-and-white illustrations, reproduced by a special offset printing process, possess a subtlety of tone, a sharpness of detail and a surface luminosity that can usually be found only in the most meticulously prepared original photographic prints.

Tice focused on Paterson in 1967 after completing a photographic series in California and another in the Pennsylvania Dutch farm country. He returned to New Jersey—where he was born and makes his home—saturated with the flamboyant coloration of California and the lush, unspoiled green of rural Pennsylvania. The somberness of his native state seemed overwhelming. "Here was time-colored country, almost an ancient civilization, and the atmosphere which enveloped it was predominantly gray." Grayness, he felt, permeated all the urban East, and he began to search for a city that would best convey this somber appearance. Newark, his home town, he knew so well that he feared its familiarity might cloud his perception. Hoboken seemed incomplete, a mere adjunct to its neighboring metropolis, New York. And New York was simply too big for his purpose.

Finally he settled on Paterson. Once a flourishing mill city, it is now grim and its population is dwindling. But it retains two arrestingly beautiful topographical features: Garret Mountain and the Passaic River falls. Nestled in this natural beauty, Paterson gave Tice the impression of a partially burnt-out lump of coal dropped into a setting of gold.

Tice set about making his portrait of Paterson in his customary meticulous manner. The project took four years. Most of the time he used a heavy 8 x 10 view camera. Lugging his equipment and setting it up—on rooftops, on street corners, in shops and in people's homes—was a demanding task, and rarely could he make more than five exposures in a day. He made the prints with similar painstaking care. For maximum sharpness, all but a few enlargements from 35mm film were contact printed from the 8 x 10 negatives and are reproduced in actual size in the book.

The result is an affectionate but candidly critical portrait of a city, warts and all. Every tar-paper shingle, every discarded beer can is sharply outlined. With only a few exceptions, the pictures are practically devoid of life: the streets, houses and shops seem to have been evacuated—not suddenly, but gradually, over the years. Even last-minute shopping on Christmas Eve looks like a grim, lonely business. Tice's Paterson has not suffered a single, devastating disaster; it has sunk into decrepitude. Its people have departed because of the lure of bigger cities nearby, or because of the attractions of a softer life in the New Jersey suburbs; without its businessmen, its builders and its children, Paterson is creeping toward premature old age.

PATERSON
Photographs and introduction by George A. Tice. 107 pages. Rutgers University Press, New Brunswick, New Jersey, 1972. $17.50.

An unwanted relic—a 10-year-old hotrod—waits ▶ for a prospective buyer, but there is no one around even to read its advertisement. Nothing in this April picture is alive; there is not a face in a window or a leaf on the trees. On a wall, a "For Rent" sign indicates that even the tenement house is to a certain extent empty of living beings.

Car for Sale, 1969

Jean's Millinery, April, 1971

All the traces of life—the equipment of a going ▶
business, the morning paper well thumbed—are
present in the picture at right; a splash of sunlight
even gives a first impression of cheeriness. Yet
by excluding people from the scene, Tice depicted
the shop as an abandoned place, as though Joe
and his customers had fled—perhaps years
ago—at the warning of an impending disaster.

An array of elaborate hats adorns display stands
and the bland-faced head of a plaster dummy, but
there seems to be no promise of customers
although a flamboyant sale announcement ought
to attract them. Jean's Millinery, like so many of
Paterson's businesses, large and small, was
suffering from the decline that has ruined
shopkeepers in many of America's central cities.

Joe's Barber Shop, December,1970

Elliott Erwitt: "Photographs and Anti-Photographs"

Photographs and Anti-Photographs is the first book devoted solely to what Elliott Erwitt calls his personal work. Erwitt, one of America's most versatile photographers, works as both photojournalist and advertising photographer, and has won fame for pictures of subjects as diverse as the Nixon-Khrushchev "kitchen debate" and the whiskey ad showing four roses embedded in ice. But during his 20 years of professional picture taking, Erwitt has also continued to treat photography as a hobby. In his own mind he is two photographers: one works for other people, tailoring his shots to their needs; the other chronicles people and places from a slightly eccentric point of view, purely for his own enjoyment. *Photographs and Anti-Photographs* is the work of the second Erwitt.

Although some of the pictures in this book are poignant and others are surreal, most are as imbued with humor as the one at right. Erwitt is one of photography's few comic artists. Some of his pictures are amusing in a gentle, delicate way; others have a tough, brash humor that provokes outright guffaws—and often the wit is less in the scene than in the eye of the beholder. The smiles evoked by the sight of a gaggle of geese, tail feathers atwitch, sharing a country lane with a cluster of ruffle-skirted schoolgirls *(page 213),* are smiles created by Erwitt himself out of ordinary visual materials. The "anti-photographs" of the title of his book refers, in fact, to pictures in which nothing seems to be happening—until one looks closer. And then the smile begins to spread.

Humor, the most conspicuous trait of these pictures, is also the most conspicuous trait of Erwitt's personality. It kept his spirits up during early struggles through penniless years and it kept his feet on the ground after he became professionally successful. Erwitt began taking pictures as a teenager in Hollywood in the mid-1940s, supporting himself not with photography but by running a boardinghouse for his friends—to whom he fed horse meat and cheap wine for 19 cents a head. Later he found work in a photographic laboratory that mass-produced pictures of movie stars, where one week he "washed and dried 25,000 Ingrid Bergmans." When he first moved to New York in 1948, he lived through what he terms his "spaghetti phase"—named for the one affordable staple of his diet—until gradually circumstances improved. From photographing authors for book jackets, he moved on to working on photographic documentaries for corporations and philanthropic foundations. During the Korean war, he converted his tour of duty in the Army Signal Corps into his first big photographic success, shooting a story on barracks life that he called "Bed and Boredom." It won him a $2,500 cash prize from LIFE. He has since explored many different techniques and subjects—including underwater photography, movies and architectural photography—but as his new book proves, he has never lost his sense of humor.

PHOTOGRAPHS AND ANTI-PHOTOGRAPHS
Photographs by Elliott Erwitt. Introduction by John Szarkowski. Biographical text by Sam Holmes. 107 pages. New York Graphic Society, Greenwich, Connecticut, 1972. $15.

All Saints Day, Paris, 1949

Wearing the masks of movie comedians Stan Laurel and Oliver Hardy, a pair of Parisians confronts the young photographer in an open marketplace as amused bystanders watch. The photograph was taken on All Saints Day— Halloween—when false faces are as common a sight in the streets as real ones.

Dummy, Wilmington, North Carolina, 1950

*Like André Kertész (page 187) and George Tice
(page 206), Erwitt is bemused by the irony
of lifeless dummies staring from windows at
humanity. Here, naked and armless, a dress-store
mannequin seems intent on getting a good view of
passersby, while a woman looks back toward the
plaster figure as though she heard someone call.*

210

In Key West, 1968

Riding in a tourist beach buggy in Florida, Erwitt photographed this odd juxtaposition of two pairs of vacationers. In the foreground, a mother and her child sit huddled and bundled as though they were taking a winter tour of a polar icecap, while in the distance two bathing-suited men sprint along the sun-baked sands at the shore's edge.

211

Heron and Friend, Florida, 1968

Two slender figures—a heron and a water faucet
—stand like nonidentical twins on a Florida
beach. The viewer is presented with a comical
paradox typical of Erwitt's visual trickery: is this a
plumbing fixture modeled to emulate the
imperious attitude of a bird? Or is the bird simply
assuming the mundane shape of a water faucet?

Sunday In Hungary, 1964

Attired in their best traditional dresses, and with every hair combed and braided, a gaggle of prim Hungarian girls share a country road with an equally proper-looking party of Sunday strollers: 17 stiff-necked, close-beaked geese. Erwitt encountered this whimsical scene while taking pictures for a book about Eastern Europe.

Other Books

Of the photographic books published in 1972, the editors especially recommend the following.

The Arts

OBSERVATIONS ON AMERICAN ARCHITECTURE
By Elliott Erwitt and Ivan Chermayeff. Viking Press, New York. 144 pages. $16.95. The authors' favorite buildings, from Colonial to modern, across the United States.

THE PAINTER AND THE PHOTOGRAPHER
By Van Deren Coke. University of New Mexico Press, Albuquerque. 324 pages. $32.00. A survey of the kinship between painting and photography, and the influences of each on the other.

THE PHOTOGRAPHS OF THOMAS EAKINS
By Gordon Hendricks. Grossman Publishers, New York. 214 pages. $30.00. Photographs that the famous painter took in order to study his subjects.

Documentaries

THE AMISH PEOPLE OF THE SOIL
By John M. Zielinski. Photo-Art Gallery, Kalona, Iowa. 85 pages. $6.00. An intimate portrait of the Iowa branch of the Amish.

GREEK PORTFOLIO
By Constantine Manos. Viking Press, New York. 128 pages. $12.95. Village life in contemporary rural Greece.

IN A SACRED MANNER WE LIVE
By Edward S. Curtis. Barre Publishers, Barre, Mass. 149 pages. $15.00. A reissue of photographs from the photographer's 1898-1930 studies of the American Indians, divided according to their native regions.

THE LINES OF MY HAND
By Robert Frank. Lustrum Press, New York, N.Y. (Distributed by Light Impressions, Rochester, N.Y.) 106 pages. $7.95. The photographer's documentation of U.S. life from post-World War II to the 1970s.

THE NORTH AMERICAN INDIANS
By Edward S. Curtis. Aperture Inc., Millerton, N.Y. 100 pages. $5.95. Another collection of Curtis's Indian photographs, many reproduced from his original negatives. Printed in gravure.

STREET TIME
By Richard Balzer. Grossman Publishers, New York, 128 pages. $3.95. Community life in New Haven's ghetto.

Personal Portfolios

ASSIGNMENT
By Snowdon. William Morrow & Co., New York,

130 pages. $12.50. Photographs by Lord Snowdon taken on journalistic assignments.

PAUL CAPONIGRO
Light Impressions, Rochester, N.Y. 80 pages. Hardbound $8.50, softbound $4.95. A second, revised and enlarged edition containing 62 of the photographer's favorite pictures.

DOUBLE TAKE
By Bill Binzen. Grossman Publishers, New York. 63 pages. $3.95. A random collection of whimsy and pathos. Most of the photographs were made by combining two transparencies or negatives —hence the title.

ECHOES OF SILENCE
By Philip Trager. Scroll Press, Bridgeport, Conn. (Distributed by Light Impressions, Rochester, N.Y.) 12 pages. $14.95. A bound portfolio of 12 landscapes and portraits, printed in gravure.

FRIDAY NIGHT IN THE COLISEUM
By Geoff Winningham. Allison Press, Houston, Tex. (Distributed by Light Impressions, Rochester, N.Y.) 144 pages. Hardbound $17.50, softbound $7.95. A study of wrestling matches in Houston.

H-I-D-I-N-G
By Fred Escher. Light Impressions, Rochester, N.Y. 28 pages. $2.50. A humorous visual hide-and-seek game, the object being to find the photographer in the landscape.

THE JOURNEY OF THE SPIRIT AFTER DEATH
By Duane Michals. Winter House, Ltd., New York. 64 pages. $3.95. A sequence of fantasy references.

MOVING ON HOLDING STILL
By Peter Simon. Grossman Publishers, New York. 176 pages. $4.95. A surrealistic view of contemporary life from Middle America to hippieland.

PHOTOGRAPHY "72"
By the Lexington Camera Club, Lexington, Ky. 60 pages. $5.00. A collection of student and semi-professional photographs.

WOMAN
By Edward Boubat. Aidan Ellis Publishing Ltd., Henley-on-Thames, England. 143 pages. £4.80 (about $12.00). Portraits of women in different countries and cultures.

Photojournalism

THE CONCERNED PHOTOGRAPHER 2
Edited by Cornell Capa. The second volume in a projected series. Grossman Publishers, New York.

176 pages. $14.95. Includes the works of Bruce Davidson, Ernst Haas, Hiroshi Hamaya, Donald McCullin, Gordon Parks, Marc Riboud, W. Eugene Smith and Dr. Roman Vishniac.

THE FACE OF ASIA
By Henri Cartier-Bresson. Viking Press, New York. 207 pages. $16.95. Portraits and way-of-life studies made by the photographer over 20 years of travel in the Orient.

MARGARET BOURKE-WHITE
By Theodore M. Brown. Andrew Dickson White Museum of Art, Ithaca, N.Y. 136 pages. $7.50. A combination biography and retrospective collection of the noted photojournalist's work from before the Depression to after World War II.

Retrospectives

ANSEL ADAMS
Edited by Liliane De Cock, with a foreword by Minor White. Morgan and Morgan, Inc., Hastings-on-Hudson, N.Y. 160 pages. $12.00. A representative selection of Adams' work, including some little-known prints.

THE COMPASSIONATE PHOTOGRAPHER
By Larry Burrows. New York Graphic Society, Greenwich, Conn. 160 pages. Slipcased, $17.95. A 20-year range of peacetime and wartime photographs by the late LIFE photographer. Color and b/w.

PAUL STRAND
Aperture Inc., Millerton, N.Y. 384 pages (two volumes). $40.00. The catalogue issued with the 1972-1973 retrospective exhibition of Strand's work (see page 12).

Technical

GLASS, BRASS & CHROME
By Kalton C. Lahue and Joseph A. Bailey. University of Oklahoma Press, Norman, Okla. 347 pages. $7.95. A history of the 35mm camera in the United States.

ILLUSTRATED DICTIONARY OF PHOTOGRAPHY
By Duncan Backhouse, Clifford Marsh, Jack Tait and George Wakefield. Fountain Press, London. (Distributed by Morgan and Morgan, Inc., Hastings-on-Hudson, N.Y.). 101 pages. Definitions and explanations of technical terms, illustrated with diagrams in color. $13.00.

PHOTOGRAPHY
By Phil Davis. Light Impressions, Rochester, N.Y. 251 pages. $5.50. A text on the mechanics of the camera and developing and printing equipment, and how to use them.

Roundup

The year brought much news beyond exhibitions, books and equipment. In France a new museum of photography opened. In the United States an already established photography museum got an energetic new boss. Elsewhere in the United States, there was a breakthrough in the field of higher education that should lead to the training of a cadre of photography scholars, critics, teachers and curators. And a treasure trove of material owned and used by one of the most brilliant pioneers of photography was donated to the nation's best-known museum of national history. But there was bad news as well. The year saw the premature deaths of three fine photographers: two Americans and an Englishman. Their lives and work are briefly summarized on the following seven pages. As for what the future holds, on page 228 there is a list of photographic events that were scheduled, as this volume went to press, to take place around the world in 1973.

Milestones

Ralph Eugene Meatyard: 1925-1972

Ralph Meatyard was an optician who photographed on Sundays and developed each year's prints during two weeks every February, working at night in his upstairs darkroom—a routine he followed during the two decades of photography that ended with his death from cancer in May. In the annual production would be portraits of friends —the Trappist monk and author Thomas Merton, folklorist John Jacob Niles, poet Wendell Barry—nature studies and shots of his family posed in the abandoned mansions Meatyard loved.

Though his work has been described as Old South Gothic, Meatyard was born in Normal, Illinois, in 1925 and grew up there. He moved to Lexington, Kentucky, in 1950; there he bought an $85 camera and began taking pictures. In 1959 he had the first of six major shows, at Louisiana's Tulane University. National recognition followed, and his work is included in the collections of the Smithsonian Institution and New York's Metropolitan Museum of Art.

The people in Meatyard's surrealistic images are often enigmatic, occasionally sinister. The casual manner of a woman striding out of the rotting wall of an old house *(previous page),* shopping bag in hand, enhances the mystery of who she is and what she is doing. A child holding a broken glass up to hide his face *(right)* portrays a secretiveness that seems unnatural in one so young. In the picture on the opposite page, light streaming into a dark, polished interior reveals a gravely watching little boy and, in the shadows, the outlines of his younger brother *(far right)*—both Meatyard's sons modeling for their father's pictures, as they often did.

Untitled, 1961

Little People, 1957

Tony Ray-Jones: 1941-1972

Tony Ray-Jones, a luminary among the young wave of photographers who established new directions for the art in the 1960s, died of leukemia in March at the age of 31. Though mainly a documentary photographer, his approach to reportage was poetic. "Photography can be a mirror and reflect life as it is," he said, "but I also think that it is possible to walk, like Alice, through a looking glass and find another kind of world with the camera." In the pictures shown here, all taken at popular English seaside resorts, his camera found a bleak, vaguely disillusioning world behind the surface allure of holiday spots. At right, the romantic promise of the elaborate decoration is belied by the middle-aged couple beneath it, the woman's eyeglass frame and the man's profile giving them a mocking resemblance to the billboard lovers. Opposite *(top),* a gloomy hotel broods over hardy beach parties on a headland. At bottom, a few determined souls, come to enjoy what guidebooks call "the bright and bracing air" of Brighton, huddle in canvas chairs against winds sweeping over the lonely beaches and deserted, once-merry amusement piers.

Ray-Jones was born in Wells in England's southwest country; he studied graphic design in London, and came to the U.S. in 1961 at age 20 to take graduate studies at Yale. There followed five years of work in New York City, as a magazine art director and freelance photographer. From 1966 to 1970 Ray-Jones worked in Great Britain and Europe, but by mid-1971 he was back in the U.S., teaching and photographing in California. He returned to London early in 1972, shortly before his death.

Blackpool, 1968

Newquay, 1968

Brighton Beach, 1968

Arthur Rickerby: 1921-1972

Art Rickerby, who started a distinguished career in photojournalism by recording the surrender of the Japanese aboard the battleship U.S.S. *Missouri* while serving as a young sailor in World War II, died in August 1972 at the age of 51. Bitten by the camera bug while still a schoolboy in New York City, Rickerby had worked his way through North Carolina's Duke University as a freelance. Soon after graduation in 1942, he joined the Navy and was assigned to the famed photographic unit that, under the direction of then Navy Captain Edward Steichen, covered World War II in the Pacific.

After the war, Rickerby worked a global beat, first for United Press and later, from 1961 to 1970, for LIFE. In 1962 and 1963 he was LIFE's White House photographer, covering John F. Kennedy's administration.

When the President's wife made a goodwill trip to India and Pakistan, Rickerby went along, and took time out from photographing the heads of state to get human-interest shots. At right, a Pakistani woman, fully veiled in public according to Moslem custom, droops with fatigue over her sleeping child while waiting to meet the First Lady at a garden reception. Opposite *(bottom),* curious citizens peer over a wall to catch a glimpse of Mrs. Kennedy.

A few weeks later, during a White House crisis involving the steel industry's attempt to raise its prices, Rickerby took a shot full of the quiet tension that filled the air during that episode *(opposite, top):* the President is speaking on the telephone at his desk while his brother Robert, then Attorney General, stares out the window.

Rawalpindi Reception, 1962

The President's Office, 1962

Pakistanis, 1962

Miscellany

Exhibition Room at the Maison de la Photographie

Tribute to Niepce

Tourists with an interest in the history of photography can add a new name to their list of places to visit. In April the town of Chalon-sur-Saône in eastern France, the birthplace of Joseph-Nicéphore Niepce, the country gentleman and inventor who took the first true photograph around 1822, celebrated the 150th anniversary of his achievement by opening a photographic center and museum, the Maison de la Photographie. Chalon has not been exactly indifferent to its famous native son in the past: a gigantic stone monument on the highway close to Niepce's estate advises the motorist, "In this village Nicéphore Niepce invented photography in 1822." Niepce's statue stands in a Chalon square, a short distance from the Avenue Nicéphore Niepce. However, the Maison now offers a far more substantial tribute to the memory of the inventor. A graceful 17th Century building that had been a postal station, the Maison's interior will not be fully renovated for several years. But two exhibition rooms, one of which is shown in the photograph above, were made ready and opened to the public in time for the inauguration.

On permanent display is a large collection of souvenirs of Niepce's life and work. It includes the cameras he used, some of them improved by inventions of his own. Three such are shown in the picture at upper left on the opposite page. A camera with a Niepce-invented iris diaphragm is at top; it is resting on a folding camera, which is alongside the earliest camera with a spool for holding a roll of sensitized paper.

Niepce used his cameras to take what he called heliographs (sun prints), a group of which are also on display at the Maison. He made his first heliograph by exposing an asphalt-coated pewter sheet for eight hours on an upstairs windowsill at his rural family estate, four miles south of Chalon. The result, now owned by the Gernsheim Collection, London, was a shadowy picture of his farmyard. It showed the grainy but discernible outlines of a prosperous 19th Century country seat: a dovecote, barn roof, bakehouse and a wing of the main house. Today, camera buffs on pilgrimage to the estate see a very different view from the same windowsill *(opposite, upper right):* outlying buildings have long since come down, and the trees that have grown up in their place have become venerable.

One of the most beautiful of Niepce's surviving heliographs was on display at the Maison's opening; it is the picture shown on the bottom of the opposite page. This image, owned by the Société Française de Photographie, in its present state resembles a Picasso still life, and is believed by some experts to have been made before the farmyard scene. But since it is a still life and since in 1829 Niepce began working with Louis Daguerre—the inventor of the first really practical photographic process, daguerreotypy, and a man who was inordinately fond of still lifes—other authorities argue that the picture was taken around that time.

Niepce's eldest brother Claude was also an inventor, and among the memorabilia in the Maison are plans for devices the brothers collaborated on.

Together they produced a pedal-less, foot-propelled bicycle and an internal-combustion engine. But the challenge of fixing photographic images by chemical means was what claimed most of their effort. They began experimenting as early as 1793, though after 1816, when Claude moved to Paris, Joseph worked alone. Tragedy struck when Claude went insane, and Joseph was forced into debt trying to care for him. Unable to get financial backing for his experiments, Joseph formed a partnership with Daguerre the year Claude died. The modest, aristocratic Niepce and the flamboyant, bourgeois Daguerre were an oddly matched pair, and other than correspondence they seem to have had little actual contact with each other. In any case, the alliance was short-lived: Niepce died in 1833, four years after it had begun.

In 1839 the government of France awarded Niepce's son Isidore a life-long pension in recognition of his father's work with Daguerre. Isidore himself made no contribution to the still-experimental art of photography, but in 1847 Abel Niepce de Saint-Victor, Joseph's cousin, invented a process using glass plates coated with a silver compound suspended in egg white as a photographic base. His process was enormously significant to the history of photography because it demonstrated the practicality of glass plates.

Present at the ceremony dedicating the Maison was a dark-haired, slender young woman in a chic pants suit. She was Janine Niepce, who is descended from an uncle of Joseph's and who is the only member of the family to carry on its tradition—Mademoiselle Niepce is herself a photographer.

Niepce's Cameras

The View from Niepce's Window Today

JOSEPH-NICÉPHORE NIEPCE: *La Table Servie*, date unknown

A First for Princeton

The United States got its first endowed professorship of the history of photography in July, when Peter C. Bunnell was named to the newly created post at Princeton University. Princeton has thus become the first school where a student can earn a Ph.D. in art history with emphasis on photography through a combination of classwork plus a dissertation. (At a few schools, such as Yale and the University of New Mexico, graduate degrees in art history can be obtained with a dissertation or thesis on a photographic subject, while classwork remains within a more usual art history curriculum.) The professorship at Princeton, funded by a one-million-dollar endowment, is named the McAlpin Chair, for investment banker David Hunter McAlpin, an alumnus with a special interest in photography, who had earlier established a series of lectures on the subject at the University.

Bunnell, a 34-year-old graduate in art history, is the former curator of photography at New York's Museum of Modern Art. He teaches his subject within the context of all 19th and 20th Century cultural and art history, since, he says, "it belongs to a community of the arts." The new professor conducted his first course—a graduate seminar on Alfred Stieglitz and the Photo-Secessionists, for which nine students enrolled—undaunted by being, so far, the only teacher in his program. His aplomb was quite in character: as Jerry Uelsmann comments about his composite portrait *(right),* "Pete is used to opening up new areas. That's why I placed him in an open doorway, and under the statue of Romulus and Remus, who founded a whole new city—Rome."

JERRY UELSMANN: *Peter Bunnell,* 1970

New Man at Eastman House

One of the world's leading photographic museums, the International Museum of Photography at George Eastman House in Rochester, New York, got a new director in December—the latest of three to hold the post in five years. He is 48-year-old Robert J. Doherty, former head of the fine arts department at Kentucky's University of Louisville, and a man of unusually varied experience: as a printing production manager, an automobile tool engineer, a graphic designer and author of a book on aluminum foil design. His versatility may aid him in holding a position that has been called "a hot potato." Clashes over the exhibition policy at the Museum—with certain factions backing the work of contemporary or little-known photographers and others a more academic approach—have made the job, according to one former director, "equivalent to running a national park."

A Windfall—and Questions— for the Smithsonian

The Smithsonian Institution in Washington, D.C., got a windfall in April: several boxes, redeemed from a family attic in a house in Pittsburgh, of memorabilia of one of the first United States photographers, the versatile scientist John William Draper.

Draper, who was born in 1811 and died in 1882, was a chemist, physiologist, physicist and astronomer as well as a historian and philosopher. As a pioneer photographer, he worked during the 1840s with his fellow professor at New York University, the artist and telegraph inventor Samuel F. B. Morse, to perfect daguerreotypy. In the collection donated to the Smithsonian by two brothers who are descendants of Professor Draper, John and James Christopher Draper, is a wide assortment of photographic equipment: wooden cameras, glass plates, daguerreotypes and a microscope. The microscope is of particular importance, for Draper was among the first photographers to make photomicrographs—pictures of objects that are so tiny they cannot be seen by the unaided eye, and must be photographed through a microscope. A label on the Smithsonian's microscope identifies it as the one Draper used in his ground-breaking work.

The daguerreotypes include many photomicrographs, a few of them magnifications of the dried blood of frogs, and one *(below, left)* a cross section of an elephant hair. Where and how Draper got his elephant hair is a puzzler, but there is a bigger question: why, as the collection proves, did Draper continue making photomicrographs on daguerreotypes as late as 1856, when the quicker and more convenient wet-plate process had been around and increasing in popularity since 1851? Smithsonian curators can only speculate that when Draper was working on his scientific studies, he feared to abandon a medium in which he was skilled for one that he understood less well.

Another mystery centers around a daguerreotype of a sober-faced young woman wearing a ruffled bonnet *(below, right)*. She is Draper's sister Dorothy, who so believed in her brother's genius that she used the money she earned teaching painting to send him through the University of Pennsylvania. Her picture, which Draper made in 1840, has long been famous as the earliest daguerreotype portrait still extant. Ruined in 1933 through a restorer's error, it was re-restored in 1969.

What intrigues the Smithsonian people is whether *their* daguerreotype is a copy of an original or a copy of a copy. The only thing they are reasonably sure of is that it is not a long-lost "real" original. Though a fine likeness, it lacks the sharpness and clarity of detail that were hallmarks of the daguerreotype.

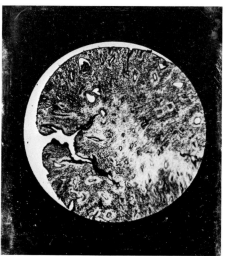

A Draper Photomicrograph, 1856

Draper's Sister Dorothy, 1840

Calendar

Photographic exhibitions, meetings and other events of 1973 are listed below according to the city and the month in which they will take place. Exact dates within each month should be ascertained from the sponsors of the events.

JANUARY
ASPEN, COLORADO Center of the Eye: Two-week seminar on color magazine photography; Four-week classes on the history of photography (through March).
CARMEL, CALIFORNIA Friends of Photography: Exhibition, Manuel Alvarez Bravo retrospective.
ESSEN, GERMANY Folkwangschule: Exhibition, "The Technique, The Picture, The Document."
FLORENCE, ITALY Gruppo Fotografico: Exhibition of competition winners.
HAMBURG, GERMANY Staatliche Landesbildstelle: Exhibition, Lotte Jacobi retrospective.
MUNICH, GERMANY Münchner Stadtmuseum: Photographs by Ernst Haas.
NEW YORK CITY Museum of Modern Art: Photographs by Diane Arbus; Exhibition, "Iconography of the Picture Press" (through April); Photographs by Mark Cohen.
Cooper Union: Photography lecture series (through April).
American Society of Magazine Photographers: Lecture by Paul Strand.
SAN FRANCISCO San Francisco Museum of Art: Exhibition, Don Worth retrospective (through March).
TORONTO, CANADA Royal Ontario Museum: Toronto Focal Forum, members' exhibition.
TURIN, ITALY Galleria Civica d'Arte Moderna: Exhibition, "Arte e Fotografia" (through February).

FEBRUARY
HAMBURG, GERMANY Staatliche Landesbildstelle: Photographs by Herbert Bayer.
NEW ORLEANS Society of Photographic Scientists and Engineers: Tutorial seminar on micrographic science.
NEW YORK CITY Metropolitan Museum: Exhibition, Paul Strand retrospective (through mid-April).
American Society of Magazine Photographers: Panel discussion, "The Photographer's Conscience."
New York Press Photographers Association: Exhibition.
PROVIDENCE, RHODE ISLAND Rhode Island School of Design: Photographs by E. J. Bellocq, "Storyville Portraits" (through March).
TORONTO, CANADA Royal Ontario Museum: Photographs by Leo Touchet, "Jazz Funeral."

MARCH
ALBUQUERQUE, NEW MEXICO University of New Mexico: Society of Photographic Education, national meeting; Exhibition, Eliot Porter retrospective.
BERKELEY, CALIFORNIA University of California Art Museum: Exhibition, "The Third Rome: 1870-1950."
HAMBURG, GERMANY Staatliche Landesbildstelle: Photographs by Walter de Mulder.
NEW YORK CITY American Society of Magazine Photographers: Panel discussion, "Taxes."
Society of Photographic Scientists and Engineers: Tutorial seminar, "Photographic Industry Marketing and Forecasting."
TORONTO, CANADA Royal Ontario Museum: Exhibition, Cavouk Portraits by Artin Cavoukian (through mid-April).
WASHINGTON, D.C. Washington International Salon of Photography: Competition exhibition.
Smithsonian Institution: Opening of renovated and enlarged Hall of Photographic History.

APRIL
CHICAGO Museum of Contemporary Art: Photographs by Diane Arbus.
CORAL GABLES, FLORIDA University of Miami: Wilson Hicks International Conference on Visual Communications.
FLORENCE, ITALY Palazzo Vecchio: Exhibition, "Documentiamo Firenze e la Toscana" (tentative).
GENOA, ITALY Gruppo Fotografico: Exhibition of competition winners.
HAMBURG, GERMANY Staatliche Landesbildstelle: Photographs by Willi Beutler.
NEW YORK CITY American Society of Magazine Photographers: Panel discussion, "Advertising Photography."
SAN FRANCISCO San Francisco Museum of Art: Exhibition, Manuel Alvarez Bravo retrospective (through June).

MAY
BOSTON Boston Center for the Arts: Exhibition, "Photovision '73."
HAMBURG, GERMANY Staatliche Landesbildstelle: Exhibition, "Hamburg: City and People."
NEW YORK CITY American Society of Magazine Photographers: "Adults Only," photographs and films on pornography.
OAKLAND, CALIFORNIA Oakland Museum: Exhibition, "Roots of Contemporary Bay Area Style."
ROCHESTER, NEW YORK Society of Photographic Scientists and Engineers: 26th annual conference.
TORONTO, CANADA Royal Ontario Museum: Exhibition, "Meteorological Optics."
WARSAW, POLAND Society of German Photographers: Exhibition (tentative).

JUNE
ASPEN, COLORADO Center of the Eye: Seminars and workshop (through August).
HALIFAX, NOVA SCOTIA Camera Canada College: Weekend workshop with guest lecturers, for nonprofessional photographers.
NAPLES, ITALY Federazione Italiana Associazioni Fotografiche: Annual congress.
NEW YORK CITY American Society of Magazine Photographers: Short films.
TORONTO, CANADA Royal Ontario Museum: Photographs by Emrie/Kotulsky (tentative); Photographs by Edward Miller (through July).

JULY
ARLES, FRANCE Festival d'Arles: Exhibition, Paul Strand (tentative); Conference, "Teaching of Photography."
TORONTO, CANADA Royal Ontario Museum: Exhibition, "Lalibela" (photographs of a monastic town in Ethiopia).
YORK, ENGLAND International Colour Association Conference: "Colour '73."

AUGUST
SAN FRANCISCO Photographic Society of America: Annual convention.

SEPTEMBER
MILAN, ITALY Salone Internazionale Cine, Ottica, Fotografia: Biannual photo fair and exhibit.
SAN FRANCISCO San Francisco Museum of Art: Exhibition, "Los Angeles Photographers" (through October).
TOKYO, JAPAN Society of Photographic Scientists and Engineers: 13th International Colloquium.

OCTOBER
ASPEN, COLORADO Center of the Eye: Classes in the history of photography (through November).
BALTIMORE, MARYLAND Baltimore Museum of Art: Photographs by Diane Arbus.
COLLEGE PARK, MARYLAND University of Maryland: Conference, "Visual Communications Today."
PADUA, ITALY Fotoclub Padova: National photography exhibition.
SAN FRANCISCO DeYoung Museum: Exhibition, Paul Strand retrospective (through January, 1974).
TOKYO, JAPAN Ueno Art Museum: Exhibitions by Nikakai and Kokugaki Art Associations.
TORONTO, CANADA Royal Ontario Museum: Exhibition, "Photographs of a New Guinea People."
TURIN, ITALY Società Fotografica Subalpina: Exhibition of competition winners.

NOVEMBER
LEVERKUSEN, GERMANY German Society for Photography: Conference, "Color."
NEW YORK CITY Metropolitan Museum of Art: "Landscape/Cityscape" (photographs by 20th Century American photographers from the museum collection).
PARIS, FRANCE Biennale de la Photographie (tentative).

DECEMBER
HAMBURG, GERMANY Staatliche Landesbildstelle: Photographs by Elli Marcus.

Bibliography

General
Lecuyer, Raymond, *Histoire de la Photographie.* S.N.E.P.-Illustration, 1945.
Pollack, Peter, *Picture History of Photography.* Harry N. Abrams, 1969.
*Taft, Robert, *Photography and the American Scene.* Dover Publications, Inc., 1938.

Special Essays
Agee, James, and Walker Evans, *Let Us Now Praise Famous Men.* Houghton Mifflin Company, 1941.
Baldwin, Sidney, *Poverty and Politics: The . Rise and Decline of the Farm Security Administration.* The University of North Carolina Press, 1968.
Bourke-White, Margaret:
  Dear Fatherland, Rest Quietly. Simon and Schuster, 1946.
  Halfway to Freedom. Simon and Schuster, 1949.
  Portrait of Myself. Simon and Schuster, 1963.
  Shooting the Russian War. Simon and Schuster, 1942.
Caldwell, Erskine, and Margaret Bourke-White:
  Say, is this the U.S.A. Duell, Sloan and Pearce, 1941.
  You Have Seen Their Faces. The Viking Press, 1937.
Duncan, David Douglas:
  I Protest! The New American Library, 1968.
  The Kremlin. New York Graphic Society, 1960.
  **Picasso's Picassos.* Harper & Row, Publishers, 1961.
  The Private World of Pablo Picasso. Harper & Row, Publishers, 1958.
  Self-Portrait: U.S.A. Harry N. Abrams, 1969.
  This Is War! Harper and Brothers Publishers, 1951.

Yankee Nomad: a photographic odyssey. Holt, Rinehart and Winston, 1966.
Haas, Ernst, *The Creation.* The Viking Press, Inc., 1971.
Kertész, André:
  (ed.), *On Reading.* Grossman, 1966.
  —and George Davis, *Day of Paris.* J. J. Augustin, 1945.
  —and Pierre MacOrlan, *Paris Vu Par André Kertész.* Librairie Plon, 1934.
  About Kertész:
  Fáróva, Anna, ed., *André Kertész.* Grossman, 1966.
  Szarkowski, John, *André Kertész: Photographer.* The Museum of Modern Art, 1964.
Ralph Eugene Meatyard, photographs. with notes by Arnold Gassen and Wendell Berry. Gnomon Press, 1970.
Strand, Paul:
  —and James Aldridge, *Living Egypt.* Aperture, Inc., Horizon Press, 1969.
  —and Basil Davidson, *Tir A'Mhurain.* Aperture, Inc., Grossman Publishers, 1968.
  —and Claude Roy, *La France de Profil.* Éditions Clairefontaine, 1952.
  —and Cesare Zavattini, *Un Paese.* Giulio Einaudi editore, S.p.A., 1955.
  About Strand:
  Newhall, Nancy, *Paul Strand: Photographs 1915-1945.* The Museum of Modern Art, Simon and Schuster, Inc., 1945.
  Paul Strand: A Retrospective Monograph, the Years 1915-1946 (Vol. I) and *The Years 1950-1968 (Vol. II).* Aperture, Inc., 1971 and 1972.

Annuals
British Journal of Photography. Henry Greenwood & Co., London, England.
Color Photography. Ziff-Davis Publishing Co., New York City.
Das Deutsche Lichtbild. Verlag DSB, Stuttgart, Germany.
Modern Photography Annual. Billboard Publications, Inc., New York City.
Photography Annual. Ziff-Davis Publishing Co., New York City.
Photography Directory Buying Guide. Ziff-Davis Publishing Co., New York City.
Photography Year Book. Fountain Press Ltd., London, England.
Popular Photography's Woman. Ziff-Davis Publishing Co., New York City.
SLR Annual. Haymarket Publishing Group, London, England.
U.S. Camera Annual. U.S. Publishing Corp., New York City.

Periodicals
Aperture, Aperture, Inc., Millerton, New York.
British Journal of Photography, Henry Greenwood & Co., London, England.
Camera, C. J. Bucher Ltd., Lucerne, Switzerland.
Camera 35, American Express Publishing Corp., New York City.
Creative Camera, Coo Press Ltd., London, England.
Infinity, American Society of Magazine Photographers, New York City.
Modern Photography, Billboard Publications, Inc., New York City.
Popular Photography, Ziff-Davis Publishing Co., New York City.
SLR Camera, Haymarket Publishing Ltd., London, England.

*Also available in paperback.

Acknowledgments

For assistance given in the preparation of this edition of PHOTOGRAPHY YEAR, the editors thank:

In the Americas—Doon Arbus, New York City; Gabriel Austin, Chief of Book Department, Sotheby Parke-Bernet Galleries Inc., New York City; Erol Baykal, Gallery of Photography, North Vancouver, British Columbia; David E. Beach, Senior Supervising Development Engineer, Eastman Kodak Company, Rochester, New York; Dennis Bradbury, Spectrum Gallery, Tucson, Arizona; Norman Bringsjord, Brooklyn, New York; Peter C. Bunnell, McAlpin Professor of the History of Photography and Modern Art, Princeton University, Princeton, New Jersey; Carolyn Carrier, Documerica Project, Environmental Protection Agency, Washington, D.C.; Theo Chunn, The Floating Foundation of Photography, New York City; Walter Clark, Rochester, New York; Erik Colonius, Documerica Project, Environmental Protection Agency, Washington, D.C.; Donald A. Dery, Director, Publicity and Communications, Polaroid Corporation, Cambridge, Massachusetts; Ann Dietz, Quivera gallery, Albuquerque, New Mexico; Michael Edelson, Contributing Editor, *Camera 35,* New York City; Cliff Edom, University of Missouri School of Journalism, Columbia, Missouri; Bill Edwards, Light Impressions, Rochester, New York; Barbara Fischer, Sotheby Parke-Bernet Galleries Inc., New York City; Mrs. Jane G. Frank, Wittenborn and Co., New York City; J. P. Gocker, Program Director, Eastman Kodak Company, Rochester, New York; Art and Emily Grice, Mind's Eye gallery, Vancouver, British Columbia; Gifford Hampshire, Director, Documerica Project, Environmental Protection Agency, Washington, D.C.; Michael Hoffman, Publisher, Aperture, Inc., Millerton, New York; Marvin Israel, New York City; Helen Johnston, Focus Gallery, San Francisco, California; Harold Jones, Light gallery, New York City; Laura Jones, Baldwin Street Gallery, Toronto, Ontario; H. M. Kinzer, Consulting Editor, *Popular Photography,* New York City; Randolph Laub, Ohio Silver gallery, Los Angeles, California; Edwin H. Land, President of the Polaroid Corporation, Cambridge, Massachusetts; Dennis Longwell, Assistant Curator, Department of Photography, The Museum of Modern Art, New York City; Tom Lovcik, Curatorial Assistant, Department of Photography, The Museum of Modern Art, New York City; Michael Lynch, Bird in Hand Galleries, Alexandria, Virginia; Christopher T. Mattson, Quality Control Engineer, Eastman Kodak Company, Rochester, New York; Mrs. Ralph Eugene Meatyard, Lexington, Kentucky; Irving Mehler,

Customer Relations Department, Honeywell Photographic Products Division, Long Island City, New York; David E. Monks, Technical Assistant to Superintendent of Consumer Assembly, Eastman Kodak Company, Rochester, New York; Henrique de Macedo Netto, Fotoptica gallery, São Paulo, Brazil; Beaumont Newhall, Visiting Professor of Art, University of New Mexico, Albuquerque, New Mexico; Eugene Ostroff, Curator, Photographic Department, Museum of History and Technology, Smithsonian Institution, Washington, D.C.; Fred R. Parker, Executive Director, Friends of Photography, Carmel, California; Conrad J. Presma, Center for Photographic Studies, Louisville, Kentucky; J. Leslie Quigley, Manager, Consumer Products Engineering, Eastman Kodak Company, Rochester, New York; Lee Romero, SoHo Photo Gallery, New York City; Arthur Rothstein, New York City; Tennyson Schad, Light gallery, New York City; Bennett T. Scheuer, Gallery Obskúra, Coconut Grove, Florida; Steven Schoen, The Floating Foundation of Photography, New York City; Maggie Sherwood, Director, The Floating Foundation of Photography, New York City; Carl Siembab, Siembab Gallery, Boston, Massachusetts; Dennis Simonetti, Albertson, New York; Michael D. Sul-

livan, Corporate Information Department, Eastman Kodak Company, Rochester, New York; Lionel Suntop, Light Impressions, Rochester, New York; John Szarkowski, Director, Department of Photography, The Museum of Modern Art, New York City; Randy and Kathleen Thomas, Mind's Eye gallery, Vancouver, British Columbia; Cummings Walker, The F/Stop gallery, Palo Alto, California; Richard R. Wareham, Divisional Vice-President, Polaroid Corporation, Cambridge, Massachusetts; Henry Wilhelm, East Street Gallery, Grinnell, Iowa; Marion and Julius Williams, The New Gallery, San Francisco, California; Lee Witkin, The Witkin Gallery, New York City; LeRoy Woodson Jr., Washington, D.C.; John M. Zielinski, Kalona, Iowa.

In Asia—Natsumi Kamigori, Tokyo Photo Gallery, Tokyo; Machiko Katagiri, Tokyo.

In Europe—Jeanne Balduin, Deutsche Gesellschaft für Photographie, Cologne, Germany; Augusto Baracchini-Caputi, Livorno, Italy; Pierre Bel, Director, Galérie Nikon, Paris; Carlo Bertelli, Director, Gabinetto Fotografico Nazionale, Rome; Adolfo Cellini, President, Società Fotografica Subalpina, Turin, Italy; Lanfranco Colombo, Director, Il Diaframma gallery, Milan, Italy; Guido Cosulich, Pictogramma gallery, Rome; Vic

Coucke, Secretary General, Europhot, Brussels; Francesco C. Crispolti, Pictogramma gallery, Rome; Sue Davies, The Photographers' Gallery Ltd., London; Michele Ghigo, President, Federazione Italiana Associazioni Fotografiche, Turin, Italy; Raymond Grosset, Director, Agence Rapho, Paris; L. Fritz Gruber, Director, Photokina, Cologne, Germany; Fritz Kempe, Director, Staatliche Landesbildstelle, Hamburg, Germany; Guy Knoché, Secretary General, Association des Gens d'Image, Paris; André Laurencin, Curator, Musée Denon, Chalon-sur-Saône, France; Jean-Claude Lemagny, Curator, Photography Department, Bibliothèque Nationale, Paris; Paul-Viktor Mackensen, Deutsche Gesellschaft für Photographie, Cologne, Germany; Alfredo Mantovani, President, Circolo Cine Fotografico, Como, Italy; Gustavo Milozzi, President, Fotoclub Padova, Padua, Italy; Allan Porter, Editor-in-Chief, *Camera*, Lucerne, Switzerland; Anna Ray-Jones, London; Christiane Roger, Administrative Secretary, Société Française de Photographie, Paris; Otto Steinert, Folkwangschule, Essen, Germany; Peter Turner, Assistant Editor, *Creative Camera*, London; Jürgen and Margaret Wilde, Album-Fotogalerie, Cologne, Germany.

Picture Credits *Credits from left to right are separated by semicolons, from top to bottom by dashes.*

COVER—Polaroid SX-70 photograph by Inge Reethof, superimposed drawing by Nicholas Fasciano; Judy Dater.

Major Shows: 11—Paul Strand. 13—Alfred Stieglitz, courtesy Paul Strand—Robert F. Haiko. 14—Paul Strand, copied by Al Freni, courtesy Columbia Broadcasting System. 17 through 33 —Paul Strand. 36 through 45—Diane Arbus, courtesy Doon Arbus. 47—Gerd Spans, Düsseldorf. Pages 48 through 53 are copyright *Camera*, Luzern. 48—Bernard Plossu. 49—Manuel Baumann. 50—Georges Tourdjman. 51—Jörg Diehl. 52—Duane Michals. 53—François Robert. 54—Mirella Ricciardi, from *Vanishing Africa*, published by Morrow, U.S.A. and Collins, U.K. 55 —Sacha, © *The Sunday Times*, London. 56 —Christa Peters. 57—Sarah Moon. 58—Charlotte March.

The Documentary: Pages 61 through 78 except page 62 are courtesy E.P.A.-Documerica. 61—Bill Gillette. 62—Ben Shahn, photograph taken for the Farm Security Administration, courtesy Library of Congress. 64—Charles O'Rear. 65—Gene Daniels. 66—Blair Pitman. 67—Marc St. Gil. 68—Blair Pitman. 69—Bill Shrout. 70—C. David Hiser. 71 —Charles O'Rear. 72—LeRoy Woodson Jr. 73 —Bill Gillette. 74—Danny Lyon. 75—Ken Heyman. 76,77—Marc St. Gil. 78—Charles O'Rear.

The New Technology: 81—Wolf von dem Bussche. 82,83—Drawing by Mary Farnberg. 85—Dick Richards (3); Polaroid SX-70 photograph by Dick Richards. 87—Polaroid SX-70 photograph by Inge Reethof. 88—Wolf von dem Bussche. 89 through 92—Drawings by Nicholas Fasciano. 93—Polaroid SX-70 photographs by Inge Reethof except top left Polaroid SX-70 photograph by Marie Cosindas. 94,95—Al Freni. 97—Courtesy Eastman Kodak Co. 98,99—Al Freni. 100—Lee Hassig. 101—Courtesy Eastman Kodak Co. 102—Courtesy Asahi Optical Co. Ltd., Tokyo; courtesy Yashica Co. Ltd., Tokyo. 103—Courtesy Canon Inc., Tokyo—Hiroshi Yokoyama. 104—Al Freni; courtesy Arel Inc., St. Louis.

Discoveries: 107—Jack Welpott; Yasuhiro Ihara —Judith Toth; Robert Ricker. 109—Naomi Savage —Joan Murray—Dwight Hooker—Oliviero Toscani —Arthur Siegel—Ann Treer. 110—Jack Welpott. 111—Judy Dater. 112 through 115—Judy Dater, courtesy Witkin Gallery. 116,117—Judy Dater. 118 through 125—Yasuhiro Ihara. 126—Judith Toth. 127 through 133—Carl Toth. 134—John Banasiak. 135—Robert Ricker. 136 through 142—John Banasiak.

The Marketplace: 145—Harald Sund. 146—Guido Cosulich. 147—Duane Michals—Claire Steinberg. 148—Lars Speyer—Harald Sund. 149—Tom McCarthy —The Floating Foundation of Photography. 150—Claire Steinberg. 151—Edward Holmes.

153—Al Freni. 154,155—David Douglas Duncan. 156,157—Leslie Krims © 1972. 158,159—Geoff Winningham. 160 through 162—George Krause.

The Annual Awards: 165—Larry Burrows for LIFE. 167—Robert Madden, for *National Geographic Magazine*. 168—Ernst Haas. 169—World Press Photo 1972 by Wolfgang Peter Geller. 170—United Press International Photo by David Kennerly. 171 —Wide World Photos by Horst Faas and Michel Laurent. 172—Guillaume Lieury. 173—Pierre Le Gall. 174—Hisaharu Taga; Kon Sasaki. 175 —Kazuo Kitai—Buko Shimizo. 176—Regina Relang © Foto Relang.

The Year's Books: 179—© André Kertész. 181—© André Kertész—Nancy Crampton. 183 through 197—© André Kertész. 199—Margaret Bourke-White for LIFE. 200 through 203—Margaret Bourke-White, courtesy LIFE. 205 through 207—George A. Tice. 209 through 213—Elliott Erwitt from Magnum.

Roundup: 217 through 219—Ralph Eugene Meatyard. 220,221—Tony Ray-Jones. 222,223 —Arthur Rickerby for LIFE. 224—Photo G. Picard. 225—Pierre Boulat for LIFE (2)—Joseph-Nicéphore Niepce, copied by Pierre Boulat for LIFE, courtesy Société Française de Photographie. 226—Jerry N. Uelsmann, courtesy Peter Bunnell. 227—J. W. Draper, courtesy Smithsonian Institution.